Endgame
in South Africa?

Endgame in South Africa?

THE CHANGING STRUCTURES &
IDEOLOGY OF APARTHEID

ROBIN COHEN

Professor of Sociology & Director
Centre for Research in Ethnic Relations
University of Warwick

Africa World Press, Inc.

P.O. Box 1892
Trenton, New Jersey 08607
(609) 695-3766

Africa World Press, Inc.
P.O. Box 1892
Trenton, N.J. 08607

First American Edition 1988

Typeset by Selina Cohen in association with
Oxford Publishing Services

Library of Congress Catalog Card Number: 88-70604

ISBN: 0-86543-090-X   Cloth
       0-86543-091-8   Paper

First published in 1986 by the United Nations
Educational, Scientific and Cultural Organizations
and
James Currey Ltd.

List of Tables

Contents

Preface

I write as Saracen cars and mounted cavalry circle the black townships of urban South Africa. A State of Emergency has been declared. Two dozen people have died due to political violence in the last fortnight, over 1000 during the last fifteen months. Some might be tempted to think this is the usual pattern of repression. It is not. For the first time since the accession to power by the National Party in 1948, the political initiative has been wrested from the hands of the government and passed to those who oppose the system. Proactive forward strategies by the theorists and planners of apartheid, have been replaced by reactive *ad hoc* measures designed to contain the spreading conflict. One of the most notable internal sounds of alarm was sounded in May 1985, when thousands of copies of a pamphlet written by a National Party MP were officially distributed to party workers. The author (van der Merwe 1985: 12) appeared to jettison great chunks of apartheid orthodoxy, arguing *inter alia* that:

> It has long been clear that political rights cannot be withheld from black people for ever . . . Large numbers of black people (as many as 60 per cent) will not be able to be accommodated physically or politically in the homelands and will, therefore, have to exercise their political rights in South Africa.

Does this *volte-face* mean that the long-predicted revolutionary explosion is about to occur? I have always been doubtful that the endgame of social and political change in South Africa can be interpreted in terms of a single cataclysmic event. When future historians periodise our time, I believe they will fix on the Soweto riots of 1976 as a 'break event', after which and despite many reversals and setbacks over a prolonged period, direct political representation and participation by the black majority in the central organs of the South African state became inevitable. Given this view, this book has an artificial quality. It provides a snapshot when only a movie camera would be adequate to capture the historical sweep, pace and trajectory of the unfolding South African drama. To reflect this sense of fluidity I have tried both to analyse those elements of stasis in the social structure that are so deeply embedded that even quite major ideological and political shifts will not easily dislodge them, and also to show where ideology and social practice are more amenable to adaptation and even quite dramatic shifts in direction.

My thanks go to Marian O'Callaghan of the Division of Human Rights and Peace at Unesco for commissioning this book, to Heather Lynn and Selina Cohen for bibliographical help, to John Bennett of Unesco for suggestions for revisions and to James and Clare Currey for their enthusiastic support.

R.C.
Centre for Research in Ethnic Relations
University of Warwick
December 1985

1 Apartheid as Ideology

As all social scientists know, the term 'ideology' is an elusive one. At a descriptive level, it may refer simply to a reasonably coherent set of assumptions and convictions that seem to be shared by an identifiable social group. Pacifists or vegetarians would hold or proclaim an ideology in this sense. But there is also, even in the loose descriptive use of the term, an element of proselytising and tub-thumping. The newly-appointed Chief Executive of the British Vegetarian Society, for example, threatened 'to make meat a thing of the past by the end of the twentieth century' (*The Times* 28 March 1985). There is something rather engagingly over-the-top about such a proclamation – but, however attractive an ideological pronouncement may be, many sensible, ordinary folk seem to want to fight shy of too close an involvement with those in the grip of an ideology, as if such unfortunates were carrying an infectious disease and needed a wide berth.

This suspicion of ideology by the many appears to have something to do with the level of commitment and conviction characteristically shown by the few to 'their' ideology. Suspicion also seems to increase with the obscurity or narrowness of the ideology. It is difficult thus to imagine economic prescriptions like Keynesianism or monetarism having large followings, though such sets of ideas have strongly influenced small, though powerful groups of politicians, industrialists and bankers. In such cases the number of adherents to an ideology is not an adequate measure of its success.

However, in the case of proselytising religions or social movements like socialism, the ideology allows only total conversion of all humankind as an acceptable index of success. Thus, the totalising and universal ideological claims of socialism, or its presumed consecutive stage communism, are well known. Yet, linking the term ideology to socialism or communism would not be recognised, indeed would be scorned, by those pristine historical materialists who see such movements as inevitable stages in world history or even as existing achievements by brave vanguard parties systematically reordering the social relations of production and reproduction. The denial that socialism or communism are ideologies also rests on their status as outcomes of a supposedly scientifically-derived theory of society. In nineteenth century marxist vocabulary, ideology is largely a denunciatory term confined to bourgeois belief systems. Whereas capitalists are mystified by ideology, socialists are supported by science.

The general scepticism surrounding the notion of, and adherence to, an ideology is therefore derived both from commonsense understandings and (amongst other traditions of thought) by the marxist heritage. Indeed, classical marxists go further than conventional wisdom in suggesting than there is an element of deliberation in the obscuring effects of an ideology. Ideology is thus not only counterposed to science, it is linked to interest. Those who pronounce their belief in Capitalism or (say) Protestantism are not simply deluding themselves, they are consciously trying to pull the wool over the eyes of those whom they wish to exploit. While marxists often imagine that they alone treat ideology in this way, it is in fact a well-established tradition for the opponents of a social movement to suggest that the real intentions of the leadership are concealed by 'ideology' or (more damning yet) 'mere ideology', while proclaiming their own beliefs as 'scientific' or (in more modern parlance) 'pragmatic'. Napoleon's polemic against the 'ideologists' first started this kind of derogatory use (Giddens 1979: 165).

Belief systems are thus subject to an intriguing play and counterplay as they enter the real social, political and economic world. Mannheim (1936) tried to universalise this observation by suggesting that the process of contesting one's adversaries' ideas turned the analysis of ideology into raw material for a 'sociology of knowledge'. Though such a notion can enthrone relativism to almost ridiculous heights, Mannheim's account often resounds with the observed cut and thrust of ideological debate. If, for example, one only wishes to pity one's opponents, their beliefs are labelled utopian or idealistic i.e. all right in their way, but not for such sophisticated urbane people like oneself. But if held convictions approximate verisimilitude, or appear to be more threatening, a more guarded response emerges. One could, for example, damn with faint praise – as in my description of the Vegetarian Society's aims as being engagingly exaggerated. Or one could indicate a certain measured acceptance of an aspect or part of what is normally seen as a unitary ideology – as in the expression 'they do have a point there'.

This last process creates particularly bitter forms of encounter and resistance. On the one hand, the partly-convinced outsider wishes to fragment and disaggregate an interlinked set of convictions, in other words to turn an ideology into a number of separable ideas, possibilities or hypotheses. On the other hand, the follower asserts that there can only be totalities, not fragments. Especially unwelcome are smart-alec or half-hearted observers rupturing a seamless web of certainty. If disaggregation of an ideology proves impossible and the ideology looks as if it might have a significant appeal, a rich depository of epithets can be assembled and deployed to damage it. An ideology, for instance, can be easily dismissed as false, racist, fascist, isolationist, adventurist, reformist, elitist, sexist, individualist, collaborationist, exclusivist or revisionist. And that by no means exhausts the list of possibilities.

APARTHEID: WHAT KIND OF IDEOLOGY?

Where does apartheid fit into this abbreviated lexicon of the nineteenth and early twentieth century discussion of ideology? In short, not very well: does it, like Mormonism or Protestantism, have a religious foundation? Protagonists for apartheid certainly do use biblical symbolism and a number of commentators have pointed to Calvinism as a powerful constituent ingredient. But though supporters of apartheid often evoke God and morality in their cause, none presents it as a substitute for religion or think of it as having a religious status in itself. Nor does apartheid have a priesthood, an elaborated doctrine, or a ritual code. To resolve this paradox, one scholar (Moodie 1975: 276) ingeniously described apartheid as a 'civil religion', defined in these terms:

> Civil religion denotes the religious dimension of the State. As such it is invariably associated with the exercise of power and with the constant regeneration of a social order; it provides a transcendent referent for sovereignty within a given territory. The ultimate nature and destiny of political power is thus connoted in the symbols of the civil faith and reenacted by civic ritual.

While it is tempting to follow such a promising lead, treating apartheid as a civil religion only illuminates one of its aspects that I want to consider here. This aspect I will call, adapting Giddens (1979: 195), the 'naturalising process'. This I will take to mean the process whereby the state functionaries use apartheid to suggest to the population, particularly the white population, that the *status quo* is a reflection of a historically legitimated 'state of nature' and a wholly normal current 'state of affairs' (see later). As well as being limited to this (important) dimension, seeing apartheid as a civil religion serves to highlight its function and meaning for the ruling group, but tells us nothing about how apartheid is experienced and understood by the majority black and brown population.

If apartheid is not a religion, and can only be understood in a limited way as a civil religion, can we see it in terms of the presumed

3

antithesis of a religion, namely a science? It is the case that on many occasions Verwoerd and one or two other theorists of apartheid deemed it to have a social scientific status. Yet even ignoring the fact that social science remains a poor cousin to natural science in terms of the status of knowledges, there can be few social theorists outside South Africa who would wish to acknowledge this deformed offspring as emanating from their loins. Even within the ranks of Afrikaner intellectuals, the Director of the government-financed Institute for Plural Societies, Professor N.J. Rhoodie, claimed that by 1981 'Afrikaner sophisticates in the academic sphere do not use this concept any more. Apartheid represents a phase in South African history and we are rapidly moving out of this phase – hence the fluidity in current socio-political thinking' (cited in Rex 1981:15). Again, it is impossible to accord any scientific status to a body of political ideas that uses 'race' as its fundamental unit and predicate. Despite gradual attenuations of the language of inherited race hierarchies in favour of culturally and historically determined differences by the 'sophisticates' known to Professor Rhoodie, the overwhelming majority of white politicians, magistrates, policemen and bureaucrats continue to think and act in racial categories. The basic building block of official discourse is constituted from 'race', a fundamentally unscientific unit of analysis, as has been notably demonstrated at successive UNESCO conferences, the main findings of which are usefully summarised by Montagu (1972).

Can apartheid perhaps be alternatively portrayed as a universal message in the manner, say, of the great religions like Islam or Christianity or the more intangible universal messages like Fraternity, Freedom or Democracy? Though apartheid is often held to be a unique and deviant phenomenon, there are sometimes some rather uncomfortable resemblances to it in the social practices of other countries. South African politicians and government officials rarely miss the opportunity to clap their hands with delight at some manifestation of racial conflict in Britain, France or the USA and like to compare their migrant labour system to that of Germany and Switzerland. Such comparisons are not always as far-fetched as western liberal opinion might imagine, but it does not take much insight to see that it is in the interests of white South African politicians to use selective evidence to suggest that racial harmony is universally impossible despite many examples that point to a contrary conclusion. Besides, asserting that people of different backgrounds cannot get on with one another is hardly a universal message of the kind proposed by the great religions. Perhaps the British National Movement, the Ku Klux Klan or the followers of the French *Ordre nouveau* could find some tenuous claim to universality in the ideas of apartheid.

But the great religions or inspiring concepts I have referred to, are specifically designed to transcend prior boundaries of ethnicity, class, status and inherited power. This clearly accounts for their appeal. Apartheid, by contrast, reinforces, maintains and extends such boundaries. Even if extremist right-wing parties in Europe and America express their spiritual affinity, the proponents of apartheid are particularly careful not to seek support from such groups. The wartime association between some leading members of the Afrikaner National Party and the Nazis is a political embarrassment that needs living down, and the post-1948 politicians have wished to represent themselves as responsible mainstream allies of the Western Alliance, not a nutty fringe group. In short, apartheid cannot have a popular, let alone universal, appeal inside South Africa or outside. The perpetrators of apartheid have all the politically significant acolytes they want, or, more importantly, are likely ever to get.

If apartheid is not religion, not science, not a universal message, is it, as marxists would assume of all capitalist ideologies, and of the beast itself, a mask to conceal particular interests? This view at least seems closer to its assumed function. But one puzzling feature of this characterisation is that very few people inside South Africa, or outside it, are fooled. One of the essential attributes of a mask is that it provides a successful disguise. It is hardly plausible to argue that it is only brave and perspicacious social scientists, toiling at the frontiers of knowledge, who have brought back the news to a waiting world that apartheid is not about equalising opportunities for all ethnic groups in South Africa. As a form of concealment then, apartheid is not notably successful. Although there are always new aspects of the experience of apartheid to discover and share, if the basic message of academic researchers is that apartheid is really about the preservation of white supremacy, this alone is not particularly revelatory.

Or is apartheid not a mask in the conventional sense? Is it nearer to ritual – a pretence at concealment akin perhaps to an operatic farce, with elegantly-coiffured ladies and porcine tenors occasionally waving implausible *papier maché* butterfly masks precariously fastened to thin dowels? If this analogy holds, it is as if the advocates and practitioners of apartheid recognise that all governments are expected to have at least some form of internal and external legitimation. Admittedly, they would privately concede, apartheid is not too convincing a disguise, but a few *arias con anima* from the resident tenor should be enough for an audience comprised only of appreciative Afrikaners and tone-deaf English-speaking whites. After all, blacks cannot afford tickets to the show and for many years the international community were only dimly aware that it was being staged.

It is perhaps difficult even for informed outsiders to quite believe this depiction, but many white, brown and black South Africans will recognise it readily enough. The point to emphasise is that, unlike Fascism, Peronism or German National Socialism, performances of apartheid ideology are not constantly staged from the balconies of the city squares. This element of hysterical demagoguery and fervent belief is largely absent. Rather, such was the myopia of many white South Africans and the corrupting influence of nearly forty years of power by the governing National Party, that they imagined they could write their dialogue behind closed doors and perform only in front of an invited audience.

NEWSPEAK AND THE REALITY OF CHANGE

Black and brown South Africans are now too politically mobilised and the international community is now too sensitised for the government to continue with its old operatic farce. As a result, it is now rare to hear any government spokesperson mention the word 'apartheid'. A considerable variety of newspeak, derived from current political movements and debates in political science and sociology in other parts of the world, have now been dragooned into service to lend authenticity to the official line that South Africa's problems, though unusual in their magnitude, are being dealt with through policies other nations have adopted – though in the face of problems few other states have experienced. 'Political Independence', 'Internal Autonomy' and 'Self-determination' is what is supposed to be happening to the old 'bantustans' and 'homelands'. 'Bantu Tribes' and 'Non-Europeans' have been transmuted into 'Black Nations'. 'Section 10 Workers' and 'Illegal Migrants' have been surprised to find themselves politely referred to as 'Urban Black Communities'. As to the relations between 'Black, White, Coloured and Indian Communities' these can be seen as a form of 'Ethnic Pluralism' and can be politically ordered though 'Confederation' (where communities are geographically separated), or through 'Co-operative Coexistence' or 'Consociational Democracy', where they are less separated. (Newspeakers have apparently not caught up with the fact that the most enthusiastic proponents of consociational democracy applied their ideas to Lebanon, before that country fell to pieces.)

The proliferation of new vocabulary can be regarded as an implicit recognition by the ruling party and its organic intellectuals that the force of real events and real struggles must in turn provoke a genuine rethink of strategies and options available to their white electorate. Is this shifting language a signal that the long road from white supremacy, to white hegemony, to white partnership, to white minority protection and finally to non-racialism is seriously being embarked on? Or is this shift in language yet another cosmetic device designed to distract the opponents of apartheid, deflect its international critics and carry on business as before?

Any answer to these questions must hinge on an assessment of which elements in the social structure and in social practice are fundamental to the basic functioning of the society and which are dispensable. Apartheid as a social practice and legal requirement covers so many areas of ordinary life that it is quite difficult to decide what is or is not fundamental. No doubt, as the pace of black and brown political participation and protest quickens, many forms of apartheid that were once thought intrinsic to the system will disappear. This process of marginalising some aspects of the system is concealed by the gradually widening definition of what constitutes so-called 'petty apartheid'. Those famous park benches marked *Slegs Blankes* (Whites Only) have now disappeared in all but the most hick towns. Black, brown and white people are now allowed to marry one another, though 'mixed' couples still have a tough time trying find anywhere to live, given that the Group Areas Act is still in force. Formerly all-white public libraries are now full of black kids desperate to escape the narrow confines of a curriculum designed to turn them into zombie labourers. Many post office entrances and counters now distinguish between inland and foreign mail rather than between white or black faces. Asian and other brown South Africans have persistently 'encroached' on 'white' beaches, resulting in the abandon-ment of the attempt to classify sand racially or in some odd compromises like the provision of white, brown *and* mixed beaches by the local municipalities. The white liberal universities have quietly increased their admittance of black candidates – an implicit defiance of the model of segregated education demanded by the government.

So far we are probably in the realm of what most would recognise as authentically petty apartheid which arose historically because of primitive pollution superstitions on the part of certain whites. Having to sit in one's back garden rather than the public park will not shake the foundations of white privilege. But how about the extensive employment of black and brown women as shop assistants and in other salaried employment? Or the recognition of both the right to organise and to bargain by trade unions representing black workers? Or the concession, first of 99-year leasehold rights to urban property, followed by freehold entitlement? Or the acceptance of voting rights for the Asian and other brown South Africans, albeit to Chambers separate from the white Chamber? It may well be argued that such advances are limited, but it is more than doubtful that they can be fitted into the category of petty.

I end up then with an implicit trichotomy. *Petty* apartheid, which still provides much salt for the wounds suffered by the black and brown communities, but which can be at least formally and legally outlawed, without major systemic consequences. *Limited* conces-sions, which the regime has often to present as petty apartheid to its electorate lest they trigger a revanchist lurch to the far right, but do

have some important systemic implications. And *fundamental* structures, which if undermined will profoundly alter the current forms of
social and political organisation, leading to what is loosely (but
wrongly if it means a single event) described as 'the revolution'. This
trichotomy provides the grounds for focusing the analysis in this book
on the relationship between apartheid as an ideology and its
relationship to the fundamental structures which it both underpins
and reflects.

THE FOUR PILLARS OF APARTHEID

What then are these fundamental structures and, given my prior, and
on the whole negative, discussion of apartheid as an ideology in some
conventional senses, how can its ideological aspects and functions be
reconstituted? My starting point is to identify what I consider the four
primary structures or pillars of apartheid without which the roof and
brickwork must cave in.

The first is the restriction of the franchise and the virtual
monopolisation by Afrikaners of centralised state power – especially
its repressive and regulatory apparatuses like the army, secret services,
police and bureaucracy. These apparatuses are discussed in Chapter 4,
but I will not elaborate on state theory as such as a parallel UNESCO
volume by Wolpe (forthcoming) will be concentrating on this aspect.

The second pillar of apartheid is the enforced coincidence between
spatial and 'racial' relations. I refer of course to the corralling of large
numbers of the rural population in the 'homelands', some of which
have obtained an independence and sovereignty unrecognised by any
country other than South Africa. I refer also to the residential, business
and social segregation cemented by legislation like the 1950 Group
Areas Act.

The third pillar of apartheid is the enforced regulation of the supply
of labour to the mines, factories, farms and white domestic households. The segmentation of the labour market both by legislation and
administrative practice remains one of the most important features of
the social structure, despite a number of reforms to the regulatory
apparatus over the last few years.

The fourth and final pillar of apartheid I consider fundamental is the
regime's capacity to enforce social control in the most vulnerable
points of the structure, namely the urban areas. It is perhaps necessary
at this stage to define more precisely what I mean by 'social control' as
the term has been used 'to cover all social processes to induce
conformity ranging from infant socialization through to public
execution' (Cohen 1985: 2). Given the extensive level of state
interference in welfare, educational, health, leisure and employment
opportunities for black people, there is some sense in seeing apartheid

(at least in intention) as a total system of social control – a womb to tomb surveillance plan for the subjugated population. However, even if patterns of health, welfare and educational provision are important parts of the brickwork (to continue my architectural analogy) the whole building is being shaken by seismic shifts from below, and the master masons have to hammer in their ties and braces somewhere. These are mainly going to support the practices and institutions of urban management and administration.

At the crudest level, the police and armed services have to clear a field of fire, making sure that it is generally the rioters and not the black councillors or themselves who are shot in error. But the state has also attempted to introduce a wide range of policies and institutions to induce some conformity, or reduce dissent, in what are the most politically sensitive zones of opposition to the apartheid system, namely the urban townships that surround the big administrative and industrial centres. I will therefore include in my discussion of social control, issues of influx control, the movement from 'Bantu Adminis-tration' to a modicum of representative democracy in the Community Councils, the extension of property rights to urban residents, other measures to stabilise the urban population, and the provision of a sufficiently large stake in the system for a sufficiently large number of blacks to keep the townships quiet.

THREE IDEOLOGICAL 'FORMS' OF APARTHEID

I have now identified what I consider the four major pillars of apartheid – the monopoly of centralised political power, the ordering of spatial relations, the regulation of the labour supply and the maintenance of urban social control – and implicitly also identified three areas of concentration for the subsequent chapters of this book (I have ignored the first pillar for the reasons stated earlier). But I am not quite ready to launch immediately into description and analysis. It is necessary first to define more precisely the relationship between the pillars supporting apartheid and the ideology itself.

I have proceeded so far by posing Socratic negatives – and concluded that apartheid was not science, not religion (except in a special sense, a civil religion), not universal message, and not a particularly effective mask to conceal class interests. It is now necessary to advance a more positive definition of apartheid as ideology. To do so, I am going to adapt to my present purposes what, in *Central problems in social theory*, Giddens (1979: 193–197) described as three principal 'forms' of ideology. These are:

(a) *The naturalising process.* For Giddens, this process denies the past, its complexity and mutability, in favour of the reification of the present, suggesting both the immutability of the current state of affairs and its wholly taken-for-granted character. Though he is not, in general, sympathetic to Lukács's views he finds this passage from Lukács's *History and Class Consciousness* (1971: 93) illustrative of how the present is 'naturalised':

> Just as the capitalist system continuously produces and reproduces itself economically on higher and higher levels, the structure of reification progressively sinks more fatefully and more definitively into the consciousness of man . . . Just as the economic theory of capitalism remains stuck in its self-centred immediacy, the same thing happens to bourgeois attempts to comprehend the ideological phenomenon of reification.

This passage captures something of the ideological function of apartheid that is visible even to the casual visitor to that country, that is, what is commonly described by outside observers as a 'sense of unreality'. This sense is most acutely developed amongst whites, particularly Afrikaners, but it is not by any means absent amongst black and brown South Africans. One example must suffice to explain this curious sense of the displacement of the abnormal to the normal. For many outside observers, whites in South Africa might be expected to show high levels of guilt (given their level of exploitation of blacks) and anxiety (given that blacks are increasingly, and increasingly violently, demanding a share of the resources and goods disproportionately held by whites). Yet observers often notice the opposite. A clinical psychologist (Lambley 1980: 105,6), applying standard Rorschach tests to a sample of nurses, found some level of stress and disorganisation amongst 'English' and 'Coloured' nurses, but none at all in the Afrikaner group:

> . . . the Rorschach profiles of these Afrikaner nurses, when compared with profiles recorded in other parts of the world, were not normal. Although all my subjects were adults, their personality profiles were not the protocols of fully functioning normal adults. There was so little anxiety and so little conflict as to constitute, in fact, a pathologically low level of functioning. Most normal people need a degree of conflict and tension in their lives to act as a means of creating frustration so that tolerances and perseverance, for example, can be learned. This lays the foundation for a personality based on the demands of reality rather than on the kind of artificial reality that children face. These women showed no creativity, no energy, no evidence of non-conformism – no sign that they thought or acted or experienced emotions beyond the confines of the expectancies laid down for them by their communities.

To paraphrase Lukács, as the violent consequences of apartheid policies progressively resonated in the real world, so one of the ideological forms of apartheid sunk progressively more fatefully and definitively into the minds of the sections of the white community that support the system. The sense of naturalness and ordinariness reflected in a lack of anxiety provides one of the sources of reassurance for the dominant classes and groups and therefore constitutes one of the most important attributes of apartheid as an ideology. Such an attribute is also revealed in casual idiom, as in the Afrikaner sayings: *Alles sal regs kom* (All will be well) and *Môre is nog 'n dag* (Tomorrow is another day), characteristically blandly stated when any difficulty arises.

The only significant change I would make to the Giddens/Lukács formulation is that apartheid does not only act to endorse the present as natural, it also reconstitutes the past as a valid legitimation for the present. In this sense apartheid acts differently from the situation described by Giddens. Instead of concealing or ignoring the past to amplify the naturalness of the present, it appropriates the past and reconstitutes it deterministically as a largely timeless 'state of nature'. Hence apartheid acts as a governing mythology, naturalising both present and past. Conventional mythology states (quite contrary to the historical record) that blacks and whites have never 'mixed', and cannot be expected to live next door to each other – let alone under the same roof. This is then transmuted into a defence of current legislation or practice ruthlessly enforcing spatial segregation (against the patterns of natural settlement or labour mobility). Apartheid thus acts both to appropriate the past, and to construct the coincidence between space and race. As I explain more fully in Chapter 2, spatial segregation is thereby made to appear as a wholly natural way of managing race relations.

(b) *Representing special interests as general ones.* This ideological form is something of a rewrapping of a bundle of similar theories already referred to, for example the marxist theories linking ideology to the concealment of (ruling class) interests. Usually this ideological form is easy to penetrate in that the political and economic interests of the governing class, white capital and the white electorate are not too elaborately hidden and are kept close to the surface. This is why I earlier referred to the appearance of apartheid as operatic farce. However, there are occasions in which apartheid ideologues seek to represent special interests as general ones in a more oblique way. This more subtle variation corresponds to Habermas's (1971: 99) view that ideologies in modern societies tend to claim a technological and scientific character, while still 'keeping power relations inaccessible to analysis and to public consciousness'. In the most advanced capitalist societies this tendency is compounded, or so Habermas argues, by a sleight of hand which advances the new scientistic ideologies in the guise of a critique of ideology. This tendency is present too in South Africa, and it can be expected to grow as diplomatic pressures incline the South African government to defend its policies in pragmatic, rather than ideological terms. However, the more cunning sleight of hand identified by Habermas is found only embryonically in some academic circles in South Africa. A good example is provided in the opening address to an international conference in Cape Town on 'intergroup accommodation in plural societies'. According to the convenor (Rhoodie 1978: 2,3):

> In terms of human misery there is much similarity between the deprivation experienced by millions of people in plural societies throughout the contemporary world and that suffered by the Accadians, Assyrians and the rest as a result of group interaction at their time. In one major respect, however, we have a distinct advantage over our ancient forebears. Today we have at our disposal the scientific apparatus and sophisticated terminology to research and identify these problems . . . A global assessment of the problem syndrome under discussion reveals that we are quite well informed on both the symptoms and causes of these problems . . . Social scientists have no difficulty at all in identifying problem areas [though] finding equitable and viable solutions to these problems is an altogether different matter. The latter require systematic socio-political engineering . . .

This quote exemplifies the beginning of a technological ideology masquerading as a critique of classical apartheid doctrine (that is, it is a restatement of the old ideological tussle between science and religion alluded to earlier). Such a change in direction is important for the future and shows the lines of paradigmatic and ideological development. It is necessary to emphasise this fluidity in current political discourse, as several orthodox critiques of apartheid (for example, Bunting 1964), as well as many media accounts, have a rather crude view of the supposed immutability of the ideas supporting apartheid.

Nonetheless, for the present, one of the ideological forms still maintains a pre-scientific representation of sectional interests as general ones. Normally, the thrust of such an ideological form is to suggest (as in the situation Marx describes) that the bourgeoisie have the general interest of the society at heart, rather than their special need to accumulate capital. This formula is a little vague for contemporary South Africa – first because of the intervention of ethnicity as a variable additional to that of class. And second, because the interests of capital are concentrated in the hands of English-speaking capitalists and foreign shareholders, who are not in direct command of the state apparatus (quite unlike the classical prescription by Marx where he assumes a complete overlap of function between rulers and capitalists).

These considerations lead to a complication in my argument which allows three possibilities: (a) does this ideological form of apartheid conceal the special interests of all whites vis-à-vis the total population? (b) does it represent the special interests of English-speaking capital as coincident with the interests of all the whites? (c) does it, finally, conflate the interests of international financiers with the interests of the South African state? Without answering these questions directly, it is clear that one answer lies in looking at the historically major productive force in South Africa, namely the gold mines – and at the social relations of production that surround the mining houses. The later development of secondary industry considerably modified the patterns of labour supply and industrial relations established by the mining companies, but they provided the grid upon which the later developments were laid. The patterns of labour segmentation and the supply of labourers to the mines therefore provide a pillar of the apartheid structure which allows us to examine how the special interests of the mining companies became identified with the wider governmental and white interest. This question will be pursued in Chapter 3.

(c) *The transmutation of contradictions.* This final ideological form suggested by Giddens can be more or less taken over intact. As he observes (1979: 194), 'It is normally in the interests of dominant groups if the existence of contradictions is denied or their real locus is obscured'. It would be pretty difficult utterly to deny the existence of contradictions in South Africa; even the government is open about the difficulties faced in ruling a 'multi-racial', 'plural' or 'multi-national' society (the vocabulary is unstable). But it is certainly a common tactic for the government to seek to displace or relocate the locus of the contradictions. How you place the blame is very much a preoccupation of the supporters of the regime. The candidates are quite numerous. 'The Communists' was a good cry, till that became more difficult with the banning and exile of the party. The Church (particularly the Anglican) also has provided a potent target. Dating from early in the nineteenth century, missionaries were seen as busybodies, giving the 'natives' ideas above their station. Troublesome priests like Bishop Huddleston exposed the shocking conditions of the post-war townships, thrown together as they were, as cheap temporary housing with minimal facilities. Now that apartheid supporters have to contend with no less than an outspoken black Bishop (Tutu) who has also been given a Nobel prize, their consternation is complete. It is but a short form of psychological displacement to suggest that those who defend the victims of the apartheid state are the instigators of the trouble occasioned by the state's policies. Other candidates for displacement include 'the foreign media', 'liberals', 'communist fellow-travellers', the local anglophone press, 'the schoolchildren' (of Soweto), 'agitators' and sundry other actors – anyone, in short, who is clearly distant from the government and its supporters.

One site to test this process of the displacement and transmutation of contradictions adequately would be the description of dissent and the construction of management and control systems in the black townships. This locus and the ideological form of the displacement of contradictions will provide the subject of Chapter 4. I will conclude this study by returning to the broad theme of apartheid as an ideology, looking in particular at the extent to which the end of apartheid is signified by the important challenges to its ideological and political hegemony demonstrated in recent urban and industrial struggles.

2 Ordering Space

Some of the most challenging work connecting spatial patterns to social relations is found in the work of 'critical human geographers', one of the most notable of whom has written on 'The Spatial Divisions of Labour' (Massey 1984). After remonstrating with economists and sociologists for ignoring geography and proceeding 'as though the world existed on the head of a pin – as though it were distanceless and spatially undifferentiated' (pp. 51, 52), she continues:

> The fact that processes take place over space, the facts of distance or closeness, of geographical variation between areas, of the individual character and meaning of specific places and regions – all these are essential to the operation of social processes themselves. Just as there are no purely spatial processes, neither are there any non-spatial social processes. Nothing much happens, bar angels dancing, on the head of a pin.

Massey is correct. It is relevant that ideologies and social processes are being played out in a particular place (and over a particular period, but I do not wish to get diverted here by the historical factor). The social and political institutions that arise from these interactions are also located in that particular space. Just as technology, science and industry are particular means of subordinating nature and seeking to command it by the force of the human will, so are planning, urban, industrial and regional policy the means contrived to direct the organisation of space. There are obvious limits to each task. Physicists might split an atom; they cannot, as yet, manufacture one. Equally, natural frontiers (mountains, rivers, oceans, deserts) normally provide absolute constraints beyond which space cannot effectively be manipulated. The constraints addressed by human, as opposed to physical geography are normally more pliable, but even here broad demographic trends (fertility, mortality and longevity rates) are not easily manipulated by social actors.

How does this discussion relate to the construction of apartheid in South Africa? In an obvious but peculiarly under-discussed way, apartheid is an attempt to manipulate geographical space in the

15

interests of furthering the principal object of its designers, namely, racial segregation. As is pointed out by Western (1984), at the heart of the preference for racially segregated space is a passionate belief in 'friction theory', the argument that any contact between different races automatically will produce conflict. Such a theory of friction provided the underlying justification for the Group Areas Act passed in 1950. Though under discussion, with some amendments this key act still remains on the statute books and still serves as the basic means of marking out the territorial space shared by all groups from that exclusive to each. In introducing the bill to Parliament on 14 June 1950, Dönges, the Minister of the Interior (cited Western 1984: 115) defended its underlying principles in these terms:

> Now this, as I say, is designed to eliminate friction between the races in the Union because we believe, and believe strongly, that points of contact – all unnecessary points of contact – between the races must be avoided. If you reduce the number of points of contact to a minimum, you reduce the possibility of friction . . . The result of putting people of different races together is to cause racial trouble.

When, eight years later, the chief modern architect of apartheid, Verwoerd, succeeded to office as Prime Minister, he continued and elaborated on Dönges's theme (cited Neame, 1962: 157) as follows:

> Dr Malan said it, and Mr Strijdom said it, and I have said it repeatedly and I want to say it again: The policy of apartheid moves consistently in the direction of more and more separate development with the ideal of total separation in all spheres. Everyone realises that it is not practicable at the present moment, that it cannot be attained in a few years, but everyone realises at the same time that if you have a clear and definite ideal in view – whether you have one moving towards separate development even territorially – it can be advanced even in these times.

What is interesting about these formulations by the main apartheid theorists of the 1950s is the implicit recognition that they were flying in the face of historical developments and current realities. Dönges supports an *ideal* of minimised contact, with the implication that the Group Areas Act is necessary because the existing level of contact is excessive. Verwoerd, for his part, recognises his ideals as currently impractical and even seems rather surprised with his own daring in suggesting that the idea of territorially separate development could be advanced 'even in these times'. In fact, Verwoerd and his colleagues were conscious that their position on the lessons and trajectory of South African history was difficult to sustain – for the historical record revealed as much in the way of cultural and racial symbiosis and contact, as it did in the way of territorial autonomy and separation.

Let me try to justify this assertion, as the government's often repeated counter-assertion that South African history reveals a minimum of race contact has gained considerable currency, even amongst opponents of apartheid. It was, of course, the case that the settlement patterns of black and white South Africans were spatially distinct, the black pastoral groups spreading into South Africa from the north and north-east, with the white settlers, arriving under the aegis of Dutch mercantile capital in the mid-seventeenth century, spreading from the extreme south to the east and north-east. However, this broad settlement pattern belies the fact that the white colony at the Cape would have been impossible to sustain without the trade relations with the Khoi-khoi (Hottentots) and San (Bushmen) and the utilisation of the indigenes' labour derived from the proximity of settlement. One year after the establishment of a white colony, its leader, Jan van Riebeeck (cited Western 1981: 277), noted in his journal:

> Only last night it happened that fifty of these natives wanted to put up their huts close to the banks of the moat of our fortress, and when told in a friendly way by our men to go a little further away they declared boldly that this was not our land but theirs and that they would place their huts wherever they chose.

The small group of Dutchmen that occupied a narrow strip of the Cape on behalf of a mercantile company for 150 years arrived without their womenfolk and engaged freely in extra-marital intercourse with the local Nama and Khoi-khoi, as well as with the slaves imported from Dutch possessions in the East Indies, West Africa, Madagascar and Mozambique (Simons and Simons 1969:12). The 'Coloured' population was the result of this interaction. Marriage with slaves was forbidden before 1823, but there were numerous examples of marriages between white and free Coloured, Nama and Khoi-khoi.

As far as the country beyond the tiny Cape settlement was concerned, by the late eighteenth century the Nguni peoples (who were organised in kingdoms ranging in size from a thousand to thirty-five thousand people) had, according to Bundy (1979: 17), 'occupied much of the broad swathe of territory between the Indian ocean and the mountain ranges that lie roughly parallel to the coast (the Winterberg, Stormberg and Drakensberg), bounded in the north by the Mzimkulu River and the south by the Fish River'. The southern area became a shifting and disputed frontier zone as the Nguni successively came into contact with the Khoi-khoi, San and the white colonists, a group of whom had escaped from the narrow confines of the Cape Colony in the 1830s. Again, racial isolation was impossible and the interactions of the pastoral black and white groups (Bantu and Boer) soon took the form of a necessary exchange of commodities and labour. Both the Nguni and the white trekkers were at a modest level of technological development, the Boers' access to manufactured goods via the Cape complementing the Nguni's more sophisticated cattle and food production. Other black nations like the Swazi and Sotho also needed European guns to defend their territorial integrity success-fully.

Towards the end of the nineteenth century – after diamonds were discovered in Kimberley and gold found on the Rand – it would have been impossible to exploit this mineral wealth without the labour of the dispossessed African peasantry. (An attempt to import Chinese labour at the turn of the century ended in a political fiasco.) Later, as export agriculture grew and manufacturing industry was established, yet again the skills and the labour of blacks were essential to the viability of the former branch of capital and the hegemony of the latter.

In short, it has proved historically impossible for the various ethnic groups in South Africa to thrive (or even survive) in territorially, economically or culturally distinct segments. Nonetheless, it has become commonplace for academic commentators (for example, Rhoodie 1978; van den Berghe 1964; 1965) to analyse South African society in terms similar to those of Furnivall's (1948: 304) description of the 'plural societies' of the Dutch East Indies. There, he argued, 'each group holds by its own religion, its own culture and language, its own ideas and ways' with the different groups living 'side by side, but separately, within the same political unit'. Whether this is an adequate description of the Dutch East Indies I cannot say; however, it certainly does not adequately describe South African society. Furnivall himself accepted that the different segments of the plural society he described 'met in the market place, in buying and selling' (1948: 304) and also saw the colonial administration as a thin skein linking together the disparate units. Such a view of South Africa is mistaken and inadequate. After the British occupied the Cape in 1806, competition from other colonial powers, internal security problems, the external strategic importance of the Cape route and the later discovery of fabulous mineral wealth, meant that the colonial state was far more powerful than 'a thin skein of administration'. The levels and instances of economic, social and cultural interaction were far more intensive than simply 'buying and selling in the market-place'. Indeed, from the very early stages of black/white interaction, a 'third column' emerged which represented the symbiosis or syncretisation of black and white cultural and social institutions.

The melding of the various elements of South African society can be analysed in many areas – in language, sexual relations, forms of religion, musical expression, furniture design, architecture, educational norms and so on – but can perhaps be most quickly demonstrated by the existence (according to the latest population estimates) of 2.77 million so-called 'Coloureds', 9 per cent of the population. Next to Brazil, this is the largest absolute and relative number of 'Afro-Europeans' in any country in the world, thus testifying to the extensive existence of sexual relations across the colour line. Of course, such relations can be highly asymmetrical and exploitative, but the point I make here relates to the extent of such relations, not their quality. According to an Afrikaner senior lecturer in human genetics at the University of Cape Town, at least seven per cent of the genes of so-called 'white' South Africans are accounted for by admixtures deriving from Khoi, San, black and Asiatic peoples (Omond 1985: 25). Modern defenders of apartheid have no way of facing up to this or other such irrefutable facts of cultural and social interaction over a long historical period. Instead they deal with such issues as peculiar anomalies or, more frequently, simply by pretending they do not exist: a stance that the early apartheid theorists would not have been in a position to defend. Those scholars who depict South Africa as a plural society in the sense used by Furnivall are, in effect, lending authority to a view of South African history that even Verwoerd and Dönges did not claim.

In arguing that South Africa cannot be seen as a traditionally segmented society, I do not, naturally, dispute the fact that, with respect to residential patterns, clustering of populations differentiated by race were inherited from the early patterns of settlement described above. Rather, I wish to suggest that despite this clustering, social and commercial interaction between the communities and across them was both frequent and intensive. As mining, farming, and later secondary industry developed on a large scale, so dispossessed black peasants, migrants from many parts of the world, free slaves, a new Coloured artisan class, indentured Indians fleeing from the sugar plantations, and a dispossessed white farming class flooded into the new urban concentrations. Many areas became 'zones of transition' with people of many backgrounds, national, racial and social, choosing, or being forced, to live cheek by jowl. In Johannesburg, for instance, after the First World War 'slumyards' inhabited by recent migrants developed a form of music and popular culture known as 'marabi' – which also, according to Todd Matshikiza (cited Koch 1983: 159), designated 'the period of popular history before the effective implementation of urban segregation'. Though the majority of the slumyard dwellers were black, they were there because they were poor rather than because they were black. Relations with other ethnic groups were intimate until 1936, by which time the municipality had all but destroyed the slumyards at the behest of the political pressures mounted by white labour, urban landowners and commercial capital. Koch (1983: 159, 162) describes the slumyard culture of Johannesburg in the 1920s and 1930s as follows:

> ... there were six large yards in Doornfontein – Rooiyard, Makapan yard, Molefe yard, Mveyane yard and Brown yard. There were also a number of cottages where 'coloureds' and 'middle class' blacks lived ... Doornfontein developed a thriving beer trade because of the diversity of its population and its proximity to the white suburbs where relatively well-paid servants worked and patronized the yard shebeens on weekends ... Women actively resisted going to the municipal locations, because these were far from the European suburbs where casual work in kitchens or doing washing could be obtained – although this was not as popular as the more lucrative and convivial beer trade. Men in the yards of Doornfontein could also supplement their income by making furniture and selling it to the white-owned second hand furniture shops in the nearby suburb of Jeppe. They could also collect old bottles, tins and bags on a commission basis for a group of whites who lived in the houses adjacent to the yards and made a living by reselling these items, especially paraffin containers, to the beer brewers and slum-dwellers.

Whereas for some multi-racial societies (for example Brazil, Trinidad) such points of cultural contact and interaction are often sources of public pride and nationalist celebration, the extent and level of relations between the population groups in South Africa is systematically misconstrued by officialdom and apartheid ideologues, who instead erect a wholly mythical history of cultural distance which is said to be the main lesson taught by South African history. As argued in Chapter I, one of the major ideological functions of apartheid is to represent spatial relations as naturally coincident with ethnic divisions. The attempt to fence off urban and rural space for the exclusive use of individual racial groups is, however, nothing to do with the natural course of South African history. It is a cruel exercise in applied geography and an attempt to try to force a wholly artificial symmetry between racial and spatial categories. To observe this process at work, I will follow South African convention by showing in turn how the state sought to create and manipulate different spaces for the different 'races'.

Before separating black, from brown, from white space the apartheid planners had to solve the difficult prior problem of giving operational force to the unscientific notion of 'race'. Before 1948, social segregation rested on custom and practice. Where policy was involved, for example in restricting Indian property and residential rights in Durban (see later), the municipal authorities relied on physical appearance (phenotype) and social identification to determine who was, or who was not, Indian. After 1948, when a national and comprehensive zoning of spatial relations was contemplated, a more watertight system of classification was necessary. The Population Registration Act of 1950 was passed to systematise previously confusing and scattered legal usages and race definitions, and to stop the high incidence of 'passing' (usually from Coloured to white) once and for all. The operational criteria were appearance, descent, general acceptance and repute – though in later legislation 'habits, education, speech, deportment and demeanour' could also be taken into account.

Trying to implement the Act through the Race Classification Board produced some notable, though degrading, farces. Pencils and combs were placed in people's hair (if held by curls, the likely classification was Coloured). Thousands of people have been 'reclassified': in 1984 for example, 518 former Coloureds became white, two whites became Chinese, one white became Indian, 89 blacks became Coloureds, and five Coloured became black. One man, Vic Wilkinson, probably holds the record by having crossed the racial divide five times. He was originally classified as 'mixed', then 'European' (white), then Coloured, then white, then finally Coloured (Omond 1985: 24,5). Reference to these absurdities is sufficient to suggest that I regard the notion and practice of racial classification as obnoxious and misguided. Nonetheless, I recognise that since 1950 the South African government has largely successfully managed to hang a racial label around the necks of the overwhelming majority of the country's inhabitants. I therefore use racial categories in this book to signify official use, employing the word 'brown' to denote Indian, Coloured and Malay.

BLACK SPACE

Blacks are by far the most significant group in the population, constituting 23 million out of South Africa's total population of 31.2 million, as shown in Table 2.1 below.

By statistically eliminating the population in the four fabricated 'independent homelands' (whose independence is not recognised internationally) official figures show that blacks constitute 17.2 million out of a total population of 25.5 million. Unlike the case of the racial categories, where it is difficult to avoid using official data, Table 2.1 amalgamates the officially accepted black population of South Africa with that in the four 'independent homelands' – Bophuthatswana (1.3 million), Ciskei (1.25 million), Transkei (2.8 million) and Venda (374,000). The total space available for the majority black population is only 13 per cent of the land, much of it in a poor condition. That proportion also includes the most notorious

Table 2.1   *Population Data by 'Race'*

Black[1]	23,029,000
White[2]	4,674,000
Brown[3]	3,568,000
	31,271,000

Notes:
1. Includes estimates for the Ciskei (1981), Transkei (1981), Venda (1982) and Bophuthatswana (1982).
2. Includes all so classified including honorary Japanese whites, Chinese, etc.
3. Includes 853,000 Asians not classified as whites and 2,715,000 Coloureds.
Source: Official population estimates for 1982.

form of black segregation, the reserve. This form of spatial segregation was to become one of the distinctive marks of the apartheid state. The reserve and other forms of residential segregation in fact predate the formal implementation of apartheid after 1948, though after that date a stronger thrust was given to implementing designs anticipated in an earlier period. In addition to the reserve, I will also cover the three other major spatial constructions designed for black South Africans – the compound, the urban township and the servants' quarters.

The Rural Reserves
Turning first to the rural reserves, these were the areas where dispossessed Africans were driven by rapacious European farmers, or where African nations made their last stands against the depredations of capital. These areas were variously called protectorates (where African rulers were able to strike a deal with the British to prevent incorporation by the Boers), native reserves, bantustans, homelands, then 'independent homelands'. Native American reservations in the US and aboriginal trust territories in Australia represent similar solutions by land-grabbing settler adminstrations. However, there are some crucial differences too. Unlike in Australia and the US, even a minimal degree of paternalism was absent in South Africa. The reserves served solely as a means of corralling labour-power into a single space which could then be drawn into or thrown from the vortex of production as and when required by capital. Another distinction lies in the attempt by the South African government to use the existence of such reserves as a means for denying political rights in what are described as white areas and, by contrast, attempting to invent citizenship for urban Africans in these areas. Finally, the tissue-thin pretence at sovereignty in several of these territories allows some international opinion to be deceived into believing that theorists

of apartheid are genuinely committed to a real devolution of political power. In fact the 'governments' of even the 'independent homelands' are nearly entirely dependent on the South African state for security, defence, foreign policy and budgetary support. In 1984, the South African state paid for 76.7 per cent of Transkei's budget, 42.7 per cent of Bophuthatwana's, 71 per cent of Venda's and 82.6 per cent of Ciskei's (Omond 1985: 99). In the case of the Transkei, the first bantustan to gain its 'independence', the geographical space was virtually consolidated and Mantanzima's leadership at first reasonably well accepted by the Xhosa people in the area. However, in an assessment after the first five years of independence, Streek and Wicksteed (1981: 1,2,362) argue that:

> ... far from proving the viability of segregation, Transkei is destroying it ... the experiment in separate development is turning into a monster ... For the Brothers Mantanzima, Transkei has provided status, power and wealth; for the chiefs, a measure of the same rewards; it has led to the creation of a tight security network; but for the mass of the people, 'independence' has meant nothing except more poverty, more oppression and fewer citizenship rights ... the number of unemployed people in Transkei appears to have reached new heights. Starvation and grinding poverty are at a maximum, thousands more unem- ployed workers continue to stream into the Transkei on Administration Board orders, and the most lucrative cash crop, dagga [marijuana], has suffered a bad decline in production owing to the drought.

Despite the hopeless situation facing the Transkei, Chief Kaiser Matanzima appears to nurture imperial ambitions over his neigh- bouring bantustan, the Ciskei, his army having been trained by the former head of Rhodesia's notorious Selous Scouts (*Guardian*, 9 September 1984). In the Ciskei, which ironically contains people ethnically identical to the Transkei (therefore in itself refuting the ethnic and national theories of the government), the independence parade was initiated with a spectacular debacle on 4 December 1981 when a drunken soldier allowed the new blue and white national flag and flagpost to come crashing to the ground. The subsequent fortunes of the Ciskei have now improved owing to an imaginative attempt to use the small territorial space as a tax haven and a site for locating small factory developments on a 'mini Hong Kong' model. The Ciskei offers South African and foreign entrepreneurs massive subsidies (diverted from South African government supplements to its budget); deregulation with no minimum wages, safety regulations or pollution laws; no company tax and a flat rate income tax at 15 per cent. Further lures include 60 per cent rebate on transport costs, a 60 per cent mortgage subsidy for managerial staff and a tax grant of 95 per cent of wage bills. With these incentives nearly 200 factories have opened their doors, including companies from Israel and Taiwan (the biggest investors) but also from the United States, Britain, Holland and Spain (*Guardian,* 9 September 1985; *Sunday Times,* 2 June 1985). This modest success paradoxically comes just at the time when government spokesmen have admitted that the homeland policy has failed, and when further attempts to devolve political power to these small enclave entities have all but been abandoned.

The Mine Compound

The second form of spatial segregation I consider occurs within the area designated as white South Africa. I refer to the mine compound, which, like the rural reserve, came to symbolise the distinctive quality of black space in southern Africa. The word 'compound' sounds like an African term, but no mine compound looks anything like a traditional African kraal. Similarly, although there are vague similarities with European penal institutions, poor houses and military encampments, none of these European institutions are significantly comparable to the mine compound. Instead, the compounds represented the emergence of a unique form of residential engineering. Large cohorts of gang labour used to blast, hoist and break the immense tonnages of gold ore needed to extract the precious metal, were lodged in exclusively male hostels, usually divided by ethnic origin and carefully policed by security forces employed by the mines. Until 1969, the mines were prohibited by law from housing more than one per cent of their black labour in family housing. The remaining 99 per cent lived in individual compounds varying in size from one housing 1,002 men to another housing 8,022 men. Wilson (1972: 10) observes that the compounds 'vary from very old pre-First World War buildings with rooms housing 50 or more men living like sardines in double-decker concrete bunks to modern hostels housing between 12 and 20 men in dormitories that compare not unfavourably with those of a white boarding school'.

In addition to modernisation, some refinements of the system included provision of a company store (analogous to the American mining houses), the provision of beer halls and the introduction of collective cooking pots. However, whatever the refinements, a form of spatial and residential segregation developed which was distinctive to southern Africa. The model of compounds pioneered by the mines has also been extended to areas surrounding the industrial centres where similar hostels for single migrants have been built. The similarity with a prison was reinforced in one observer's mind by the provision of a control room outside the gates of the hostel fitted with a switchboard connected to steel doors at the end of every corridor. At a touch of a button, corridors could be sealed off and, so the planners believed, riots and strikes contained (Wilson 1972: 43).

The Urban Township

The third type of spatial segregation considered is the urban township which was constructed principally as an alternative to the spontaneous settlements that grew up on the periphery of the great commercial, industrial and manufacturing centres – principally around Johannesburg, Port Elizabeth, East London, Pretoria and Cape Town. Social scientists familiar with third world squatter settlements, for example the *favelas* of Rio de Janeiro, would not be particularly surprised to find shanty towns springing up as peasants migrate from the countryside to where they can seek work or eke out some kind of livelihood. Although the state has been unable to prevent the emergence of perhaps 1.5 million squatters, the right of residence in urban areas has nonetheless been rigorously controlled through the use of influx control measures, stop and search procedures for passes by a hostile police force, and raids for offenders who had drifted into the townships without permission.

Only a small proportion of African urban residents are housed in privately constructed dwellings. Instead, for reasons of social control (discussed in Chapter 4), after the Second World War the South African state embarked ruthlessly on evicting squatters in the name of slum clearance, and building vast lines of public housing. Despite a considerable provision, the Office of the Prime Minister estimated that another two and a half million more homes would be needed by 1990. Until 1975, the overwhelming majority of blacks were only allowed to rent property in white urban areas. Thereafter, 30-year leases were provided for some 'qualified' residents, a concession that was extended in 1978 to provide 99-year leases and then, in 1985, to freehold rights. These extensions of urban tenure are of great significance in symbolically undermining the prior rulings of the apartheid state that no blacks were to have permanent rights in white areas. However, given the low income levels of many blacks, their take up should not be exaggerated – by the beginning of 1984 only 8,000 leaseholds had been signed. The housing on offer is known as 'type 51/6', a small 4-bedroom house with outside lavatory, asbestos roof and brick or breeze-block walls. The general appearance of the townships is well described by Smith (1982: 24):

> For most of the blacks there are slots in the monotonous single-storey rows set down with the characteristic regularity of state-constructed labour storage projects – harsh repressive forms relieved only by individual human endeavour manifested in a newly painted front door, an attempt to lay a lawn, and,

occasionally, an extension or rebuilding initiative imitative of what would be found in a modest white suburb.

Servants' Quarters

The fourth arena of black space, also found commonly in slave and colonial societies, namely the provision of separate quarters for the domestic servants is widely employed in white residences. Characteristically, a separate outhouse is constructed, provided with rudimentary facilities and cut off by internal locks from the whites' sleeping areas. Police raids on the servants' quarters of white households are common with a view to discovering whether family members, not authorised to live in, are present. Even the huge skyscraper apartment blocks of Hillbrow (which provide a Manhattan-like landscape to a part of Johannesburg just north of the city centre) have been designed to ensure that separate housing provision is provided for black cleaners and cooks. Zooming up in a lift, the polished lobbies provided nearly to the top of the apartment block will suddenly give way to a concrete floor and to tiny concrete cells perched on top of the roof next to the ventilator shaft and the TV aerials. Such accommodation is quaintly referred to as a 'location in the sky'.

The compounds, the reserves, the townships and the servants' quarters are not 'natural' forms of spatial segregation. On the contrary, they are built, made, maintained, and policed by the white state often with the help of army reinforcement.

BROWN SPACE

I am using the word brown here to refer to South Africans of Indian descent (870,000 people comprising 3 per cent of the population) as well as those described in South Africa as Coloured. The word 'Coloured' is of particularly vague provenance having at one time referred inclusively to Cape Malays, Griquas, Indians, Chinese, 'other Asiatic', and 'other Coloured' (Proclamation 46 of 1959).

The argument sometimes heard, that white Afrikaners get the blame for a system that English-speaking whites support and actually helped to create, is validated not only by the mine compounds and the servants' quarters (operated by English capital and by white 'madams' of both white language groups), but also by the treatment of Indians by the Durban city authorities. Durban is the heartland of English South Africa. (Johannesburg, which rivals it in the number of English-speakers is, as far as the white population is concerned, a polyglot collection of Cornishmen, Scotsmen, Greeks, Portuguese, Jews and others who masquerade under a common ethnic identity, constructed solely from an approximately white skin colour.) The worthy English citizens of Durban, who were not at all pleased at the thought of having to live next door to successful Indian shopkeepers and merchants who had escaped their poverty on the plantations, took the lead in constructing brown space. In 1922, a City Ordinance provided for Whites Only residential areas. Indians were able nonetheless to 'penetrate' these areas using other legal means, until they were prevented from doing so following two Union government commissions established at the behest of the white Durban citizenry and then by the 'Pegging Act' of 1943. This 'pegged' the *status quo* with regard to interracial property transfers and, lest any Asian find his way out of that, a further Asiatic Land Tenure and Indian Representation Act (the so-called 'Ghetto' Act) was passed in 1946. The Group Areas Act followed four years later and, as I have noted earlier, remains the basis of spatial segregation. However, what was notable about Durban was that the City Council's Technical Sub-Committee of the City Planning Division was the first to try to establish the working rules of town planning under a spatially segregated model. Using a distorted appreciation of British town planning legislation, the Sub-Committee evolved seven principles which, as Western (1984: 118) argues, can be employed 'to deduce an ideal apartheid city'.

The seven principles were: (a) residential race zones with 'barriers of a kind preventing or discouraging contact between races in neighbouring residential zones' and transport for each zone 'so that its residents do not have to traverse the residential areas of another race'; (b) different race zones should not be juxtaposed and room for urban and employment expansion should be provided; (c) industry should be dispersed in ribbon formation in order to give the maximum length of common boundary between working areas and residential zones; (d) the present racial pattern of land ownership and occupation was 'not a material consideration', although (e) 'settled racially homogeneous communities should not be disturbed except in so far as it is necessary to give effect to the postulates set out above'; (f) the different needs of racial groups in respect of building and site development would be considered, and (g) in the initial stage the central business and industrial areas should not be earmarked for the exclusive use of any one race.

Such an ideal apartheid city is mapped by Western (1984: 121) who also shows that there is a strong presumption that the Durban principles were used as a model for the implementation of the Group Areas Act. The attempts by Mahatma Gandhi to appeal to Smuts's goodwill in respect of the 'Pegging Act' came to no avail and Durban soon took the appearance of a largely all-white city, with Indians either operating as market-place traders or acting as waiters to the large numbers of tourists who descended from the Rand to avail themselves of Durban's steamy climate.

The other part of the brown population of South Africa suffered its most notorious reverse in respect of the Group Areas Act not in Durban, however, but in Cape Town, where the principle of allowing existing racially homogeneous areas of settlement to continue was ignored in the interests of achieving some of the other postulates of race/space planning. I refer of course to the forcible displacement of Cape Coloureds from District Six in Cape Town. It is not the case, as I indicated earlier, that the Coloureds are a racially homogeneous group, but District Six was a culturally distinctive area – blending together artisanal skills, musical and artistic talents and petty trade in an attractive and original sub-culture. Unfortunately, District Six happened to be in the path of city developers and in sight of envious chic whites who saw the possibilities of turning the Malay houses into charming town residences. At the time of the accession to power by the Nationalists in 1948, the population in Cape Town comprised 44 per cent white, 44 per cent Coloured, 11 per cent black and 1 per cent Indian. As Western (1981) shows, the white planners were simply not prepared to recognise the prior claims of Coloureds to District Six – for the reasons mentioned earlier and also because Cape Town, as the 'Mother City' where Jan van Riebeeck, the sacred ancestor of the Afrikaners, first set foot, had a symbolic value as an expression of white settlement and dominance.

The brown Capetonians were ruthlessly displaced by property speculators, white 'yuppies' (young urban professionals) and government officials securing space for new city developments. They were dumped in an area known as the Cape Flats, 12 kilometres from the city, in a bleak, inhospitable, windswept environment where transport costs became a major hazard. The life of the city collapsed and the brown people of Cape Town were not able to effectively mount a challenge to the apartheid planners until the 1970s. Symbolically the movement of Coloureds from the centre of the city was also an indication that the Afrikaner had renounced them as a cognate people. It is generally the case and true of South Africa that physical distance also reflects social distance (Sommer 1969; Popenoe 1973). There are 678,000 Coloureds who are Dutch Reformed Church members and the majority speak Afrikaans as their mother language. Considerable numbers of Coloureds also 'passed' into the white Afrikaner community and were officially so registered. These strong bonds of language, consanguinity and religion were symbolically torn asunder by the expulsion of the Coloureds from District Six. It is indeed notable that many highly-placed Afrikaners are more uncomfortable about this act of vandalism and violation than anything they have done to the black population. Some of this group now talk openly of abandoning apartheid insofar as it prevents the readmission of what they call 'brown Afrikaners' to the *volk*.

WHITE SPACE

Until the recent urban disturbances when property values and a secure, comfortable life style were adversely affected even in their own areas, white South Africans enjoyed a standard of living approximated only by the residents of the more affluent areas of southern California. It should, of course, not be imagined that all whites live in the lap of luxury. A city like Johannesburg is visibly divided in respect of the housing occupied by white communities of different levels of income. Modest single-story bungalows built in the 1930s and 1940s are predominant around the south and west of the city. Such housing grew around the mining shafts and factory areas and is inhabited mainly by white miners, clerks, railway workers and others members of what would be considered a working-class in a western industrial society. Their white skin and their intermediate status as supervisors of black labour mean that such groups are better conceived as a middle-class or petit-bourgeoisie.

Within the city centre and in the apartment blocks that ring it, Greeks, Portuguese and other southern Europeans, together with students and other transient dwellers, live in solid but rarely luxurious apartment blocks. It is only as the visitor reaches the northern rim of the city that the extraordinary affluence of the economically successful whites becomes apparent. In these suburbs it is common to find a swimming pool, a tennis court, two or more family cars, large rolling lawns and flower beds and individually styled, architect-designed, double-storey houses, sometimes so large as to be considered mansions. Such dwellings, though showing an enviable level of style, design and decor, are something of a gilded cage for their inhabitants. Wrought-iron burglar-proof bars cover each window, thin wires or sonar systems are linked to alarm systems and usually connected to the 'flying squad' [the police mobile unit], while high walls and trained Alsatian dogs frequently provide further deterrents to black burglars or rapists, about whom there is often a fear amounting to paranoia. Even attendance at the palaces of conspicuous consumption – the ritzy theatres, restaurants, hotels, shopping malls and movie houses – are accompanied by a careful sidewards or backwards glance as the white couple rushes to their large car and remembers to roll the windows up tight.

As in some of the large cities of the US, the business district and the old city centre of Johannesburg, while still containing the previously fashionable department stores and boutiques, have largely become the shopping zones for discount houses and chain stores selling cheaper goods to blacks from Soweto. The fashion boutiques, *haute couture*, polished car showrooms and expensive restaurants have moved to lavish shopping complexes, lit by ornate chandeliers and cooled by waterfalls, fountains and the ubiquitous air-conditioning. In these polished monuments to consumer madness, whites on the tip of Africa's continent can convincingly pretend to be on the Champs Elysées, in Bond Street or on New York's Fifth Avenue. Black consumers are not formally forbidden to enter such treasure troves (though, until recently, they were prevented from eating at the restaurants), but there are few blacks who can find the money or the transport or brave the stares of the security guards to make use of such facilities.

Residential and consumer segregation are paralleled by the construction of exclusively white educational, health and recreational space. White children are educated both apart from their brown and black countrymen (except in the case of a tiny handful of private schools) and within a separate language (English or Afrikaans) group. Frequently, schools are also gender-specific. The insistence on racially-zoned tertiary education has not been completely achieved and there are strong indications that the major liberal 'white' universities (Witwatersrand and Cape Town) are successfully defying the government and admitting larger and larger cohorts of black undergraduates. Much health care and many clinics and hospitals are privately funded by large insurance premiums, thus ensuring their exclusive use by whites. Public hospitals for blacks are generally, though not generously, provided and often partly staffed by white doctors. However, within wards and operating theatres, a rigorous form of apartheid obtains. White doctors can probe black patients, though no black orderly, nurse or doctor is permitted to touch a white patient. Occasionally some grim humour relieves this extraordinary arrangement, as when a white patient awoke prematurely from an anaesthetic to find a black orderly, pushed into service due to staff shortages, wheeling her trolley. She screamed at this violation of her person. As with health care, many sporting and recreational facilities are racially zoned, though many of these boundaries are falling away as 'petty apartheid' comes under challenge.

FORCED REMOVALS AND THE GROWTH OF SHARED SPACE

Despite the consistent attempts by the government to eliminate 'black spots', declare more and more areas as 'reserved areas', bulldoze illegal squatter settlements, forcibly remove settled urban populations like the Cape Coloureds, zone off health, educational and recreational areas, and restrict property and business rights, by 1985 it was possible to conclude that the area of space shared between the races, for the first time since 1948, was increasing rather than shrinking. This is not to deny the extraordinary success the government has had since 1948 in trying to reverse three hundred years of mixed settlement. Using the Population Register Act of 1950, thousands of families whose racial identity was ambiguous to themselves or their neighbours have now been classified into the various decreed racial classifications. According to one source, more than eight million blacks were made citizens of the 'homelands' between 1976–1981 (Omond 1985: 101). Of course, not all of these were physically moved from 'white' South Africa, but the loss of citizenship (now under revision again in the wake of current events) meant that all citizens of the homelands lost potential entitlements to leasehold property and residential and work rights in the urban areas. They were therefore potential victims to expulsion under the pass laws and influx control regulations. The number of blacks permanently 'endorsed out' under these regulations is virtually incalculable, as many arrestees can be expected to return to their supposedly illegal place of work or residence in the face of no alternative way of earning a living in the impoverished reserves. One estimate (LL, July 1984) was that 17 million blacks have been arrested under South Africa's pass laws since the turn of the century.

Even if we put to one side this continual process of arresting, endorsing out, remigration, rearresting, etc, there is nonetheless sound statistical evidence of more permanent population removals. The most reliable count has been made by a team of researchers known as the Surplus People Project (cited Omond 1985: 114–5) who tabulated over 3.5 million removals between 1960–1983. The start date for the project implies missing a considerable number of removals, particularly under the Group Areas Act, for the previous decade. Nonetheless, it does provide the most accurate measure available, and I reproduce their data in Table 2.2 below:

Table 2.2	*Removals of Population, 1960–83*
Evictions of farm tenants and redundant farmworkers	1,129,000
Removal of 'black spots' in 'white land'	674,000
Moving urban townships from 'white areas' to homelands	670,000
Removal of squatter settlements	112,000+
Rezonings under the Group Areas Act	834,000
Removals for development schemes and security reasons	23,500
Exiles, either self imposed or state imposed	50,000
Moving resettlement areas	30,000
	3,522,500

Source: Omond 1985: 114–5.

There are two ways of reading this statistical evidence. On the one hand, it can be seen as evidence of a ruthless government determined to implement its ideological principles and showing the capacity to do so. On the other hand, the very fact of having to move so many people forcibly and to arrest millions more under the country's pass laws suggests that there is some inexorable logic promoting spatial overlap-

31

ping or integration between the races. Under this reading of the evidence the attempt to spatially segregate and segment the races flies in the face of South African history and the demands of the economy. Like King Canute, the South African government is trying to hold back the sea.

Evidence that the government has itself now concluded that its removals policy is futile is as yet fragmentary, but there is no doubt that during the last couple of years, coinciding with the period of intense political unrest, the government has not undertaken any population removals on the scale conducted during the previous three and a half decades. In May 1985, the government announced (SAN May 1985) that it had decided against the resettlement of 700,000 blacks and would instead develop the 52 urban townships, previously slated for demolition, rather than move the inhabitants to new areas. The Deputy Minister of Co-operation, Dr G. de V. Morrison, told Parliament that 'resettlements had a strongly negative effect on social structures and had become grossly politicised, both internally and abroad'. He added that 'the development of townships as permanent residential areas would strongly encourage settled community life'. Three months later, the Deputy Minister of Development and Land Affairs, Mr B. Wilkens, announced that, after negotiations with a delegation of the Kwa-Ngema black community, the government decided that the community would not be resettled. It would remain permanently on land occupied by the community near Wakkerstroom in the Transvaal and compensation would be paid for some land flooded because of the construction of a nearby dam (SAN August/September 1985).

The South African government also finally abandoned its plan to give an area called Kangwane to Swaziland, which bordered it. Kangwane was claimed by the former King of Swaziland and many of the people in this area speak Swazi. The apparent benevolence of the South African government belied the fact that the scheme would in effect be gaining tacit international recognition by awarding territory to an Organisation of African Unity member. At the same time some 735,000 blacks would lose South African citizenship. Simultaneously, the Swazi state would suffer a huge drop in its per capita income which would make her more dependent on the South African regime and more liable to take orders from its security agencies in respect of the treatment of African nationalist militants within its borders.

The collapse of the Swazi negotiations and the increased reluctance of the South African authorities to undertake mass removals are signs that the process of spatial segregation by government decree has now been halted. Instead, the amount of shared social space between the races has gradually been increasing. The log-jam started uncoupling in 1983 when President P. W. Botha suggested that unnecessary discriminatory measures that created ill feeling should be removed – though he was 'not in favour of a system of compulsory integration' (Omond 1985: 46). This opened considerable room for a modification of the Reservation of Separate Amenities Act of 1953 which provided for socially segregated civic halls, libraries, theatres, parks, cinemas, hotels, restaurants, cafes, clubs, sports amenities and beaches. Now local authorities, communities and businesses could apply for permits to desegregate many of these spaces. Most libraries, a number of international clubs, a number of cinemas, 75 hotels, most post office counters, game parks, nature reserves, pleasure resorts and many urban parks have been opened to all races.

Some of these changes of shared social space have taken an interesting 'class' form. For example, in October 1985 'specified cinemas' in the central business districts of four major cities and all drive-in cinemas were declared open cinemas, increasing the number of cinemas open to all races from 25 to 160. However, as a newspaper report (*Guardian* 8 October 1985) noted, the conservative white population would only have to adjust to this invasion of their space rather slowly as the cinemas opened were luxury cinemas with high admission fees, 'a factor which will help to prevent "flooding" of cinemas by underprivileged blacks'. A second, more absurd example arises from the elected Coloured and Indian representatives in the new parliamentary structure. Because Cape Town is a white area, special parliamentary 'villages' had to be created to provide office, housing and debating accommodation for the Coloured and Indian MPs at the cost of some £13 million!

The growth in shared social space is also seen in the behaviour patterns now observed in South African cities. Black and brown South Africans are increasingly evident in the shops and commercial areas and are increasingly reluctant to adopt a passive or cringing attitude in the face of white pedestrians or motorists. Symbols of white power and previously undeclared white space, like the City Hall steps, the central parks, the major shopping malls, the large department stores and the lobbies and restaurants of opulent hotels are increasingly occupied by black sightseers and shoppers.

The halting of further population removals and the increase in shared social space between the races have led some political commentators in South Africa to consider a fundamental realignment of the social space between the races. I shall here mention only three schemes that have attracted some discussion in South Africa, but draw the attention of the reader to the fact that political solutions in South Africa (just as in the case of apartheid itself) are often conceived in spatial terms.

The first scheme discussed was developed by Prince Buthelezi, Chief Minister of KwaZulu and leader of the powerful conservative political organisation Inkatha, with a reputed membership of over one million people. The scheme arose from a Commission set up in 1980 by Buthelezi and supported by Harry Oppenheimer, the former Chairman of Anglo-American, and representatives of organisations ranging from the Canegrowers Association and the Institute of Bankers to the Natal Teachers Society and the University of Stellenbosch. The Commission reported in 1982 and proposed, amidst a wealth of sociological data, that the homeland of KwaZulu and 'white' Natal come together to 'form a new non-radical, power-sharing political unit within South Africa . . . ruled by a joint executive committee initially made up of equal members from the KwaZulu Cabinet and from the Natal Provincial Association and subsequently appointed, on a multi-racial and multi-cultural basis, by a Chief Minister elected by a local legislative assembly' (*Guardian* 14 August 1985). Although the plan was ridiculed at the time by the government, in the wake of the urban unrest during 1985, it has gained a new wave of support. For Buthelezi, his fragmented homeland, comprising 44 separate bits of land dotted across the length and breadth of Natal, would make more geographic sense and would open a possible route to the sea, thus giving the homeland some possible economic viability and allowing him to challenge the other more radical political options available to black and brown South Africans. For nervous white opinion, 'the Natal option' as it has come to be called, would permit an experiment in territorial and social engineering which could be adopted in piecemeal and later stages in other parts of South Africa.

A second blueprint for the spatial realignment of South Africa is briefly discussed in Gann and Duignan (1981: 298,302). According to their summary, a black writer, Ngubane, proposed a Swiss cantonal federation which would have four types of states: African, Afrikaner, English and non-racial. These ethnic states would be based on existing living areas. The conflicting interests between each 'racial' group would be held in check by a constitutional device that would guarantee that no one group would dominate the others. Though Gann and Duignan upbraid their readers for not being familiar with this important book and imply that they wish us to take Ngubane's views seriously, they had themselves earlier dismissed Ngubane's multistate plan on the grounds that 'partition clearly makes no sense in an economically integrated industrial society' (p298).

Whereas Ngubane's scheme is a somewhat fanciful utopia, an even more radical proposal by a right-wing Afrikaner, Pieter Bruwer, seems more of a defensive posture constructed in anticipation of the arrival of a dystopia. Bruwer, a member of the *Oranje Werkers* (an Afrikaner organisation committed to the idea of a white homeland), like many other extreme right-wing Afrikaners, is totally convinced that President Botha is embarked on a disastrous course of reform which will inevitably result in an integrated country under black rule. The alternative they propose is to abandon great chunks of southern Africa to blacks and browns together with what they see as their 'white liberal' English-speaking friends. The new plan would provide a territorial homeland for two million out of the 2.6 million Afrikaners and would use as its historical justification the old Boer republics of the Transvaal, the Orange Free State and Vryheid. Its heartland would include the white industrial powerhouse in the Johannesburg/Pretoria area, accounting for more than half of South Africa's wealth. It would include also most of Namibia, including Walvis Bay and Windhoek and the diamond mines, but not the troubled area of Ovamboland which would form a separate black state, Namibia. A southern corridor would link the heartland to Mossel Bay, with an eastern corridor linked to Richards Bay, the fastest growing port in east Africa. Excluded from his plan is the city of Cape Town, which would form the core area of a Republic of Good Hope abandoned to the Coloureds and white liberals. Port Elizabeth and Durban would be abandoned to the black states of Xhosaland and KwaZulu.

CONCLUSION

Contrary to the official statements provided by apartheid ideologues, and their attempt to naturalise their preferred state of affairs, South Africa has never been a racially segmented society in the sense understood by such devotees. The level of intercourse between the different population groups in respect of sexual relations, commercial exchange and a complementary industrial division of labour all suggest that the apartheid scheme is ultimately doomed. As Verwoerd and his colleagues in the 1950s were well aware, what they were attempting was no less than the spatial reordering of an entire society. In terms of the level of social engineering involved, it is comparable only perhaps to the period of heavy industrialisation in the Soviet Union under Stalin or the deployment of foreign and concentration camp labour in wartime Germany. In each case a strongly repressive state apparatus had to be constructed to implement spatial changes of the type contemplated.

It is a testament to the singlemindedness of the apartheid regime in the period after 1948 that it was able to classify into largely self-constructed racial types an entire population of over 30 million people. It is equally notable that the regime was able to switch citizenship for perhaps eight million people and physically remove some 3.5 million people in furtherance of its schemes. Simply contemplating the amount of police action, transport arrangements, rebuilding, paper work and other forms of administrative dedication leaves one somewhat astonished that a regime with virtually no legitimacy amongst the black and brown people and a somewhat narrow majority electoral base (at least for the first 15 years) even amongst the white electorate was able to undertake this scale of social change. It should also be remembered that the National Party supporters comprised, for the most part, ill-educated and often poor Afrikaners (two-thirds of whom were illiterate in the 1920s) who had few administrative, technical or scientific skills.

The key to this conundrum lies in the 'naturalising' effect of the ideology of apartheid itself. What Verwoerd and his colleagues were able successfully to implant was that the fears of many whites, particularly poor Afrikaner whites, in respect of job, housing and educational competition from black and brown South Africans were totally acceptable and normal. In this sense, apartheid provided a comforting set of ideas for a group that had suffered defeat at the hands of the British during the Boer War, was humiliated by rural emiseration, awkward in the company of English-speaking whites and incapable of mounting an effective challenge to the potential social mobility of black and brown South Africans. The appeal to a common history, the creation of a distinctive national language (ironically amalgamated from Dutch and Khoi-khoi) and the strong sense of isolation as a white community, permanently stranded on an alien continent, reinforced Verwoerd's appeal to this distressed and bewildered community.

The self confidence of the Afrikaners grew under the tender care of a benevolent state. Jobs were protected for poor and unskilled whites; social welfare, generous child allowances and housing were provided; Afrikaner children were educated free and up to a tertiary level; all major administrative posts were assigned on the principle of ethnic favouritism and, finally, Afrikaner capital was nurtured at the expense of English and Jewish capital. As these forms of ethnic group mobility began to pay off, the naturalisation process inherent in the ideology was extended from a narrower definition of all Afrikaners to one of all whites – who were now jointly enjoined to celebrate the distinctiveness of their white skins. Though many English-speaking white South Africans distanced themselves from Afrikaners in terms of the assumed lower status of the latter, the long traditions of class and social snobbery, which take the form of class consciousness in the English context, were given a new meaning in South Africa and reordered as race consciousness. As most blacks were indeed workers, due to the restricted opportunities for social mobility, the coincidence between black and working class did not provide any great intellectual hurdle for class conscious English-speakers to cross.

This process of naturalisation occurred to some degree within the black and brown communities as well. For the brown community, in particular for the Coloureds, the construction of racial categories has been a wholly traumatic experience. Linked by language, religion, cultural norms and occupational similarity to the Afrikaners, their exclusion from the welfare state set up for ethnically acceptable Afrikaners propelled them virtually entirely into the hands of the black oppositional forces in South Africa. (Whether the lure of being recast as 'brown Afrikaners' has any attraction remains to be seen). As for the blacks, the doctrine of apartheid did at least permit a sense of pride in one's appearance and one's own culture, language and identity. It is therefore not wholly surprising that strong movements of black consciousness arose. Some attempted to reconstruct mythical tribal kingdoms and represented a peculiar and inverted parody of apartheid ideology. Other forms of black consciousness were more akin to those found in the US and other parts of the black diaspora. Insofar as these currents of thought gripped the minds of the black masses, they served only to reinforce the apartheid notion that separateness was inevitable, normal and typical.

Fortunately this veil of common sense, which informs white support for the regime, can no longer meaningfully be sustained. The political demands of black and brown people are many and varied, but they include a predominant strain which is pushing in the direction of equal opportunities in a unitary non-racial or multi-racial state. The stridency of such demands and their persistence, despite nearly 40 years of formal apartheid, suggests that ultimately it will be impossible to make the boundaries of race coincide with the boundaries of space. This is not to say that the massive shifts in the territorial space occupied by the different population groups will not take many years to disentangle in the event of a unitary constitution and majority democratic rule. This is an issue I return to in my final chapter.

3 Regulating Labour

A number of influential interpretations (for example, Wolpe 1972) have focused on the reproduction and regulation of cheap labour as the essence of the apartheid system, arguing in particular that post-Second World War apartheid replaced 'segregation' as an adaptation to the changing labour requirements of capital. The allocation of labour is indeed a feature of central significance. Moreover, it is one where some of the major tensions of apartheid theory and practice are revealed, as the government seeks to reconcile the countervailing and internally disparate demands of the employers, with the views of the white electorate. While white voters have been convinced that spatial and racial segregation are the only means whereby the perpetual continuance of white supremacy can be assured, those who are in command of the processes of capital accumulation (be this on the mines, farms or factories) recognise that they require considerable cohorts of cheap labour-power on the spot in order to drive the machine of production forward. Taking the cases of the mines, farms and factories in turn, I will briefly indicate their divergent need for cheap labour, before describing the nature of the labour supply system to each sector in more detail.

The mining companies have historically always depended on lowering their costs through the labour component. Until recently, mining was a highly labour-intensive operation. With a fixed price of gold operating for many years, some companies found it difficult to produce enough gold from the huge tonnages of ore it is necessary to mine, in order to compete with the more successful and better capitalised mining houses. Given the symbolic association of gold with wealth, it is readily assumed by outsiders that the mining houses have always made fabulous profits. This, however, has not always been the case. From 1935–63, the average rate of return on mining shares was 4.3 per cent, compared with seven per cent for UK equities (Frankel cited Lipton 1985: 115). Moreover, white miners, as a result of skill scarcity, the exercise of their political muscle, and their industrial militancy after the First World War, had forced the mining houses to pay them a relatively high wage.

The natural victims to low profits and high white labour costs were black workers, whose wages before 1973 either stabilised at real turn-of-the-century levels, or, in some cases, were reduced. As I will show below, this low-wage strategy for black miners was available to mining capital until recently, when a partial challenge to the labour supply points was posed by the gathering pace of African nationalism, and an internal challenge was posed by the growth of a powerful union. As to the first challenge, the mining companies circumvented this in the past by extending their field of recruitment in wider and wider circles, thus reducing market competition in the supply price of labour. As the products of gold mining were almost entirely for export (the small internal market for jewellery being beyond even a median working class wage), there were no contradictory consumer pressures to drive the mining wage upwards.

In the case of agriculture, most of South Africa's land is correctly characterised as 'agriculturally poor, with low quality soil, erratic rainfall and little natural irrigation' (Lipton 1985: 85). Many of South Africa's farmers, white and black, were driven off the land by droughts, locusts, cattle diseases and unstable world prices for their export products. At the same time, white farmers provided the bulwark of support for Afrikaner nationalism in the period after the Boer War. From the 1940s, the two major white political coalitions, the Nationalist and United parties, competed for their vote. The United Party's claims were, however, severely damaged, despite the Afrikaner origins of its leader Smuts, by its association with English-speaking mining capital. Nonetheless, farmers' support for the Nationalist party was obtained only in exchange for seemingly permanent and massive subsidies, together with the guaranteed supply (sometimes challenged by the mines) of a cheap, coerced black labour force. South Africa's export produce – like the Cape apples and Outspan oranges commonly found in European markets – could only compete in these distant markets with considerable internal subsidies, a set of marketing boards that ironed out international price fluctuations and a supply of labour available at the right price and at the right time for the ripening crop. Until blacks began to enter the market for food as significant consumers in the 1970s, it was in the interests of farmers to keep the cost of labour cheap in order best to deliver competitive goods to the export market.

Such a cross-pressured position in relation to black wage earners was faced by manufacturing and service capital at a much earlier stage. After the Second World War, when secondary industry begun to develop to a considerable degree, the factory owners were immediately aware of the need to enlarge the internal market for consumer goods, and were aware also how this need potentially conflicted with their ability to compete in world markets. On the whole, the industry that emerged could not successfully compete with Asian manufactures in the European and North American markets (however depressed the wages were), and instead opted for a predominant role as an import-substituting industry, partly nursed by import tariffs on similar goods. For such industries (footwear, clothing, textiles are examples), the initial internal market of consumers was too limited. Higher wage levels were therefore necessary both to ensure that a supply of labourers could be drawn away from the previously monopsonistic mining houses and also to create a significant black consumer market.

THE ORIGINS AND DEVELOPMENT OF THE MIGRANT SYSTEM
ON THE MINES

The demand for large numbers of labourers was manifested first on the diamond mines of Kimberley, and thereafter with the discovery of gold on the Witwatersrand reef. Black pastoralists from the surrounding areas were induced to abandon their holdings by the combination of tax demands, land grabbing and the lure of wages. The scale of changes wrought by 'the minerals revolution' can be gauged from some statistical data. Within 15 years of the discovery of diamonds in 1867, gems to the value of £32 million had been exported. By 1881, the annual export value of diamonds exceeded the value of all other exports passed through the major ports, these diamonds being produced with the aid of 17,000 black diggers (van der Horst 1971: 66, 85). The discovery of gold in 1886 was to have an even more dramatic effect on the surrounding pastoral economies of the region. By the turn of the century, just short of 100,000 labourers were employed in the Witwatersrand mines (Wilson 1972: 2).

The temporary adequacy of labour supply was soon disrupted. The Boer War of 1899–1902 caused considerable difficulties, for nearly all workers had returned to the rural areas when the mines were shut down. At the same time, a speculative gold boom fuelled the formation of 299 new gold-mining companies. The High Commissioner, Lord Milner, was desperate: 'I believe that when everything is done that can be, we shall still be short, and very short, of unskilled labour' (cited in van der Horst 1971: 168). His fears were well grounded, for a special Commission reporting in 1904 concluded that the mines needed 197,644 labourers and had only been successful in recruiting 68,280. Though 'dead against Asiatic settlers and traders', Lord Milner thought 'the indentured Asiatic would prove controllable'. Accordingly, some 66,000 Chinese indentured labourers were recruited over the next three years (Richardson 1984: 167).

The recruitment of Chinese workers was to prove a short-lived solution. Milner, as indicated, authorised it only under extreme pressure. It completely violated his grand plan to anglicise the country in the wake of the Boer War, while the Liberal Government in Britain, under challenge from humanitarian lobbies, refused licences for the further importation of indentured Chinese after November 1906. Yet, short-lived as this episode was, it demonstrated one of the laws of motion of the South African gold-mining industry. Faced with a production crisis, a tap regulating the supply of labourers from a suitable reservoir, however distant, could quickly be turned on. If reduced production or politics intervened, the tap could be turned off just as quickly.

For the political reasons indicated, the Chinese could not, however, provide anything but a stop-gap solution. In the longer run it made more sense to try to regularise the process of labour recruitment from Portuguese East Africa (present-day Mozambique). Though labourers from the East Coast already constituted 60 per cent of the total mine labour force in 1897, there was a great deal of uncertainty by the Chamber of Mines as to whether this source could be relied on. Wage rates fluctuated sharply, numerous contracting agencies tried to undercut each other to secure orders from the Chamber, the transport and security arrangements for recruits were inadequate, and Portuguese officials were often corrupted by having to deal with the rival bids of predatory labour contractors. With some exasperation the mine owners complained that, 'at Delagoa Bay everything is done by bribery and everybody from the highest to the lowest takes a bribe' (cited Levy 1982: 66). It was time for a more rational form of capital to intervene.

The Chamber proceeded to establish the Witwatersrand Native Labour Association (WENELA), the successor body to a small organisation established in 1896. In a secret deal with the Portuguese authorities, WENELA was given the monopoly over recruiting in Mozambique. There is some evidence to suggest that in addition to freezing out the Portuguese labour recruiters, WENELA was supported by the larger mining interests in order to throttle the supply of labour to the weaker companies. The small mining group, J.B. Robinson, for example, tried to circumvent WENELA's control, but the Portuguese, though pretending compliance at first, never produced a recruiting license for the company (First 1983: 18).

Though the recruitment of labour to the mines was henceforth to remain in the companies' hands, the colonial administration in South Africa (established after the Boer War), successive South African governments and the Portuguese authorities were involved in a series of inter-governmental treaties on the issue of labour recruitment. A *modus vivendi* was agreed in 1901, which led to the Mozambique Conventions of 1909 and 1928. These were amended in 1964 and supplemented by additional agreements in 1965 and 1970. Governmental interests were involved in a number of areas. The South African state was determined to maintain the temporary form of migration, insisting indeed that three-year contracts be amended to one year. For their part, the Portuguese authorities used their control over the supply of labourers to extract a deal over the routing of goods from the Transvaal through the

Mozambican ports and along her railways. The Portuguese went so far as to suspend recruitment before the colonial government in South Africa knuckled under to their demands. By 1928, not only did the Portuguese authorities obtain a guarantee of the flow of goods along their rail heads, they also acquired the revenue from a native tax, levied at the mines, and paid to Lisbon in gold.

Mozambique was to become one of the largest reservoirs for mineworkers destined for the Witwatersrand, with a share of the labour force ranging from 71 per cent in 1906 down to 10.52 per cent in 1982. The dramatic collapse of the Mozambique share was dictated by a number of interrelated events including, after 1976, the ultimately doomed attempt by the new revolutionary government of Mozambique, led by FRELIMO, to painfully and slowly try to disengage the Mozambican economy from the enveloping clutches of South Africa. Until quite recently the South African authorities and the mineowners always saw the advantage of contriving to declare a large proportion of workers coming to the mines as 'foreigners' – foreign signifying totally without rights of representation, rights of settlement or access to what few social benefits were provided within South Africa. Legassick and de Clerq (1984: 142, 143) point out that, even ignoring the ambiguities of nineteenth century territorial distinctions which pre-dated the unification of the South African state in 1910, post-union legislation was manipulated to define or redefine the category of 'foreign'. For example, the Admissions of Persons to the Union Act (22 of 1913) classified African workers from Mozambique and Malawi (Nyasaland) as 'prohibited immigrants' whose 'standards or habits of life' made them unsuitable for permanent settlement in South Africa. Such persons could only enter the country in terms of an inter-governmental treaty or approved contract-labour recruitment scheme.

The mining companies were also keen to push further northwards to recruit more and more foreigners, who were known in the recruiting trade as 'Tropicals'. These were black workers north of 22° latitude. The Portuguese attempted to restrict this recruitment to maintain their own hold on the supply. Another difficulty was the mortality rate of workers from these areas, mainly from pneumonia, which reached alarming proportions – some 67.6 for every 1,000 recruited in 1911 (van der Horst 1971: 221). It is an indication of the importance the mining companies attached to this source of labour supply that they set up and funded the South African Institute of Medical Research which developed the powerful Lister anti-pneumococcal vaccine in the 1920s to reduce the death rate of tropical labour. A major stimulus to successful recruiting in the tropical areas also lay in the provision of improved transport facilities. WENELA established recruiting stations in present-day Namibia, Botswana, Zimbabwe, Zambia and Malawi, built a 1,500 mile road linking its stations in Namibia and Botswana, established motor-barge transport on the Zambesi River and laid on train and air services to Malawi and Botswana. By 1955, there were 32 flights organised by WENELA in or out of the Botswana capital each week.

Naturally, Tropicals from all these areas were deemed 'foreign' and therefore 'prohibited immigrants'. On the other hand, workers from Lesotho, Swaziland and Botswana, that is the High Commission territories, were deemed part of a mythical entity called 'British South Africa'. This conveniently-invented designation allowed these areas to be treated as 'native reserves' in the way described in my previous chapter. It was only in 1963, when the process of decolonisation raised the imminent prospect of these territories becoming independent states, that workers from Botswana, Lesotho and Swaziland were suddenly reduced to the status of 'foreign'. The rapid dismantling of the British Empire, together with the impending collapse of Portuguese rule in their southern African colonies, was a serious threat to the mines' recruiting policy. Though the labour would continue to be 'foreign', negotiations would now have to be conducted with nationalist leaders whose rhetoric occasionally even included some threatening populist and anti-capitalist sentiments. Even so compliant a figure as President Banda was impelled by public outrage to cut off the Malawian labour supply in 1974 when a plane carrying 72 Malawian mineworkers crashed, killing all the passengers. Though supplies from Malawi were resumed in 1977, they never attained their former level.

As politics had intervened in the case of the Chinese workers, so 70 years later the force of African nationalism became a political threat to the now traditional policy of recruiting foreign workers, for whom virtually no social, political or economic responsibilities were assumed by the South African state or the Chamber of Mines. The fact that these workers were selected for their healthy appearance and signed up on short term contracts also provided considerable savings for the state in respect of the reproduction of labour-power (Wolpe 1972; Cohen 1986). Fortunately for the mines, as the supply of foreign labour looked less certain, the South African government had begun to implement its bantustan policies, by converting some of the 'native reserves' to 'independent homelands'. On this matter at least, there was no disjuncture of interest between mining capital and the apartheid state, a presumption of conflict that liberal commentary often suggests as inevitable (see Lipton 1985: 110–137). Both 'progressive' capital and the 'reactionary' state shared a common purpose in internalising the labour supply. Such a process can be clearly observed in Table 3.1.

Table 3.1   *South African and Foreign Sources*
            of Black Mine Workers (Selected Years)

	1973		1978		1982	
FOREIGN	No.	%	No.	%	No.	%
Lesotho	87,229	20.66	104,143	22.85	99,034	22.09
Botswana	16,811	3.98	18,129	3.95	18,148	4.04
Swaziland	4,526	1.07	8,352	1.83	9,422	2.10
Mozambique	99,424	23.55	45,168	9.91	47,150	10.52
Tropicals	127,970	30.32	29,618	6.50	16,262	3.63
TOTAL FOREIGN	335,960	79.58	205,410	45.07	190,016	42.40
TOTAL SOUTH AFRICAN*	86,221	20.42	250,311	54.93	257,954	57.60
TOTAL	422,181	100.00	455,721	100.00	448,170	100.00

*Includes the 'independent homelands'
Sources: Murray 1981: 30; Lipton 1985: 385.

As Table 3.1 shows, in under a decade the proportion of workers recruited from inside South Africa had nearly trebled from 20 per cent to nearly 60 per cent. For the mineowners, this fundamental shift in the historic recruitment pattern might have occasioned a collapse in profits, as it coincided with a quadrupling of wages from 1972–6 – the result of the first effective organisation and action by the mine workers since 1946. Mammon smiled on the mineowners, however, for as the world-wide recession deepened, the price of gold in South Africa rocketed from R28.60 per fine oz. in 1971 to R168.90 per fine oz. in 1978 (R1 roughly equalled US$1 over the period). Thus, despite the large increases in the wages of African workers, the profits per African employee rose from R1,485 in 1972 to R4,000 in the late 1970s (Stahl 1981: 37). From the point of view of the government, the switch towards the internalisation of the labour supply by the mines was wholly congenial to the evolution of the apartheid policy, about three quarters of the South African recruits having emanated from the Transkei and other bantustans. The availability of work on the mines for bantustan labourers also gave the temporary illusion that the homelands policy could work.

However, the rise in profit levels also provided the mines with an opportunity to seriously embark on a programme of mechanisation. New processes for the extraction of gold from the old dumps also helped to change the character of the bigger mines towards a more factory-like form of production. Most companies followed the logic of greater capital intensity by stabilising the work force. As the effects of mechanisation begin to pay off, the mines are expected to employ fewer workers, on longer contracts, at a higher rate, and in conditions that include the provision of rented accommodation and some other facilities for the miner and his family. Nonetheless, it is not planned that family wage earners will totally supersede the migrant labourers on the mines, who still remain the predominant component of the labour force.

THE LABOUR SUPPLY IN FARMING AND MANUFACTURING

Until the 1950s, the demographic pressures and rural emiseration of the reserves were insufficient to ensure adequate supplies of labour for the white farmers, who by the end of the nineteenth century had occupied and secured title to most of the land of present-day South Africa. It was particularly difficult to secure adequate numbers of labourers to work on the Natal sugar plantations, as those Africans who were prepared to work for white farmers still tried to cling on to their own property and chose to work only seasonally. The plantation owners, like their counterparts in the Caribbean, Mauritius and Fiji, imported thousands of indentured Indians to cut and mill the sugar cane. Other seasonal farmworkers were imported from outside the country – as in mining, Mozambique providing the single biggest foreign source.

The majority of rural Africans were either driven into the native reserves or became squatters or labour tenants on white farms. The system of tenancy provided for temporary and seasonal labour in exchange for a modicum of security, but many white farmers found tenant labour unsatisfactory and looked to the South African state to provide further seasonal gangs of farmworkers. One source came from the vast numbers of blacks who were arrested under the pass offences or were incarcerated for other minor offences. Farmers were permitted to bid for convict labour at the local police stations in exchange for offering food and accommodation. The conditions met by convict labourers were almost invariably scandalous – an inadequate diet, sacks used for bedding, concrete floors for beds, and brutal treatment by guards and farmers. Many of these 'convicts' were minor offenders processed in batches in the magistrates' courts, many of whom had done no more than forget their pass documents at home.

The political influence the farmers wielded also allowed them to have privileged access to the state's additional labour supply points, particularly the labour bureaux. The agricultural unions and other organisations of farmers put pressure on the government to restrict the mobility of rural blacks to the urban areas and prevent the mines from drawing on the same pool of labour. The tenancy system was reinforced by a battery of legislation, including the repressive Masters and Servants laws, which prevented absconding and sought to criminalise worker mobility. These measures prevented any effective competition for labour with the mines or with manufacturing, thus allowing large wage discrepancies to arise. In 1952 for example, average farm wages were 64 per cent of the cash wage on the mines and only 27 per cent of the manufacturing wage (Lipton 1985: 98).

From the 1960s, major economic changes affecting the farming sector propelled contradictory tendencies to the conditions existing previously – in particular these changes challenged the ultimate dependence on a cheap, coerced labour force. The rising income of blacks led to an increased elasticity of demand for food. So, like the manufacturers, discussed below, the farmers stood to gain for the first time from increased black incomes to mop up internal food surpluses. The internal rural market for food would not perhaps have been significant had the farmers' export market not also been threatened by the United Kingdom's entry into the EEC. A certain level of mechanisation also meant that the wealthier farmers were keener to use the plots occupied by squatters for their own production rather than hang onto an increasingly marginal labour force, including aged retainers and children. As in mining, the wealthier farmers as well as those whose labour costs were a small element in total costs (for example egg farmers, where labour only accounted for 7–10 per cent), could see some advantages in the development of a free labour market, even assuming that wages would rise. Amongst other benefits a free labour market conferred on such farmers was the prospect of driving their poorer competitors out of business.

In the case of manufacturing industry, the support for a free labour market, a stabilised work force and the phasing out of migratory labour has always been at the core of the industry's political demands, and the source of considerable tension with the government. Even in the 1920s and 1930s, businessmen were pressing for higher black wages, complaining that the wages of our 'principal consuming population' were too low and that 'even a slight increase' in black incomes would lead to a big increase in demand (Bozzoli cited in Lipton 1985: 161). In looking at how apartheid affects wage costs for manufacturing industry, we have to take into account certain mutually conflicting institutional pressures, given that free labour market mechanisms are severely distorted by apartheid policies.

On the one hand, by implementing influx controls and pass laws, apartheid planners prevented large numbers of workers from flooding into the towns and therefore depressing wage levels. Additionally, manufacturing wage costs were also increased by indirect means in that manufacturing capital, through levies and taxes, had to pay for the cost of implementing the system of regulation and the labour bureaux (see later). On the other hand, by restricting political rights in the towns and limiting trade union organisational possibilities, apartheid drove down wage levels and inhibited collective action for better wages. Also of significance is the number of illegal workers present in the urban areas – either falling foul of internal pass controls or external immigration restrictions. Though most of these workers are active in the informal and service sectors, some job competition with this segment of the labour force occurs within manufacturing too, again acting to force wages in a downward direction. These contradictory effects of the apartheid system have pulled business and manufacturing interests first this way then that in trying to evolve a consistent attitude to the government on questions of wage bargaining, wage costs and the recognition of black trade unions. However, with the increased organisational capacity now manifested by black workers, most manufacturers take the view that a stable, more productive and better paid labour force is necessary to the development of a bullish consumer market.

Though some countervailing arguments are mounted in relation to black wages, manufacturing capital is united in wishing to abolish the remaining racial restrictions on entering different jobs and trades. The principal legislation enforcing job reservation by race was the Industrial Conciliation Act (No. 28 of 1956) covering building, clothing, footwear, motor assembly, transport, the wholesale meat trade, road construction, some lift operators and 'barmen in white public bars'. In each of these cases, whites were given the plum jobs, while blacks were allocated to the dirty, dangerous and poorly paid ones. Black apprenticeships were restricted and even when blacks undertook 'white jobs' they were still paid at a lower rate and not given recognition for the skills they acquired on the job. In Cape Town, whites only could be ambulance drivers, firemen and traffic policemen over the rank of constable. Additionally, there were special regional restrictions that operated in Cape Town in respect of the 'Coloured preference policy' which forbade blacks to take jobs that could be filled by brown workers.

In some respects, the colour bar in industry offered a useful control mechanism for employers in that they could hold down wages by pleading 'governmental restrictions' and also take advantage of the skilled labour-time offered by black workers without having to pay commensurate wages. However, the colour bar in industry also prevented black/white wage competition and featherbedded inefficient and poorly trained white workers, leading to a good deal of shop-floor resentment. Besides, the National government by the mid 1970s, in effect, had already implemented its protective policies designed to help poorer Afrikaners adjusting to the demands of urban and industrial life. So when industry began to push at the job colour bar, they were pushing at a nearly open door.

By the mid 1980s, all major restrictions, bar one, had disappeared. The remaining bar is the granting of a blasting certificate exclusively to white mineworkers, which certificate had the effect of maintaining the distinction between high-paid skilled white, and low-paid unskilled black, miners. This exclusive privilege was won by white miner political and strike action in the 1920s, and has been fiercely clung to ever since. It is significant that this example of job reservation pre-dates the Nationalist electoral victory in 1948 and the Industrial Conciliation Act eight years later. Because it is so deep-rooted it will take all the power of black organised labour to dislodge it. Indeed, the 'whites only' blasting certificate is one of the main targets of the recently revived black mineworkers union, who will almost certainly succeed in their demand for the dropping of this restriction.

INFLUX CONTROLS, LABOUR BUREAUX AND LABOUR PROTESTS

In this section, I will be concerned with the attempts, particularly the recent attempts, by the South African state to manage and control the supplies of labour-power to South African industry, agriculture and mining, as well as the major recent protests by the workers against such interventions by the state. At the heart of the present control system is the pass – in effect, an internal passport which serves as an identity document, an indication of work and residence status, an indication of nationality (including the fabricated 'homelands' nationality accorded to most blacks) and equally importantly, a police record.

White South African officialdom is fond of using the term influx (Latin, *influere*, flowing in) to describe the movement of African labourers. The term suggests a natural, spontaneous process which has nothing to do with the almost insatiable historical demand for black gang labour by the mines or the massive recruitment drives initiated by mines' recruitment agencies and other labour suppliers. In so far, however, as an 'influx' suggests an inanimate, depersonalised phenomenon, akin to a rising tide, it would seem only right and proper that the representatives of 'civilisation' should erect dykes and canals to control this threat.

In fact, the control measures are implemented on an almost unbelievable scale. In one study, Savage estimated that since the turn of the century, 17 million blacks have been arrested under the South African pass laws. In another, West showed that about 10 per cent of adult blacks in Cape Town are likely to be arrested each year. Women are particularly likely to be singled out as pass offenders as the authorities rightly see their presence as a harbinger for the establishment of black families in the area (LL, July 1984).

The implementation of the pass and other regulations in turn depends on the status of the arrestee under the provisions established primarily by the Bantu (Urban Areas) Consolidation Act of 1946. Section 10 of that act stipulates that no African may remain in an urban or peri-urban area for longer than 72 hours unless such a 'visitor' 'qualifies' to be there. Qualification lies in continuous residence since birth (Section 10/1/a), continuous working for one employer for 10 years (Section 10/1/b) or a restricted possibility for immediate family to join a male breadwinner (Section 10/1/c). Urban residents who qualified under these provisions can be considered the permanent, stable, urban residents whom the post-1948 Nationalist Party government were forced to accept and could not be 'endorsed out' to the homelands or forced into the contract labour system. Consequently, such residents constitute the core of the black urban working class in service, domestic and manufacturing employment. The terms 'Section 10 workers' or 'Section Tenners' are often applied to such residents who have gained an entitlement to live in a black urban township like Soweto (the South Western Townships) near Johannesburg.

In fact, Section 10 also provides a sub-clause qualifying workers to stay in the urban area with the permission of a local labour bureau, the functions of which are discussed later. But as the bureaux rarely give permission to anyone other than short-term contract workers, this provision is a way of controlling migrant worker registrations, rather than permitting another route into permanent urban residence. In 1968, the Regulations for Labour Bureaux made clear that a black could not qualify for urban residence by extending an initial short contract for successive years until the 10 year period (specified in 10/1/b) was fulfilled. A succession of contracts would not be regarded as continuous service (Wages Commission n.d.: 18, 19). This ruling was successfully challenged in a fascinating court case brought by a machine operator, Mehlolo Rikhoto, which went to the Court of Appeal in 1983. The Minister of Co-operation and Development, who estimated that 143,000 migrant workers might benefit from the Rikhoto decision, decided to accept the judgement, but block the loophole by other means. He insisted that such workers and their families be housed in 'approved housing'. As there was already an officially recognised housing shortage of 260,000 houses, this provided an immediately effective deterrent to any other workers wishing to emulate Mr Rikhoto (*African Labour News* August 1983).

Labour Bureaux
In effect, the distinction between Section Tenners and contract

workers hardened into a distinction between stable and migrant labourers, the latter being routed either through the mines' private system of recruitment (already discussed above) or through the state's system of labour bureaux. It is these labour bureaux that provide the institutional basis for the classification, funnelling and further regulation of labour-power and are, in substance, replacing the politically-discredited pass system. This point is of crucial significance in understanding the reason for the government's apparent willingness (in late 1985) to consider the abolition of the pass system and influx control.

Labour bureaux have been in existence in embryonic form since the turn of the century, but their number and powers increased sharply as a result of the 1964 Bantu Labour Act, the 1965 Bantu Labour Regulations and the 1968 Regulations for Labour Bureaux. As a result of these measures, a network of 1,300 labour bureaux was provided to cover every city, town, village or rural area in the country. The bureaux, in turn, cover three types of area – 'prescribed' i.e. 'white' industrial and residential areas where Section Tenners are the predominant black labour force; 'non-prescribed', where the 'district' labour bureaux mainly supply agricultural labour to the farming communities; and 'homeland' areas. The homelands' bureaux are hierarchised into 'territorial', 'district' and 'tribal' offices, and constitute the effective base of the system.

It is important to emphasize two aspects of the homelands' bureaux. One is that they are directly accountable to the Central Labour Bureau in Pretoria, thus further exposing the apartheid myth that these areas are in some measure 'independent'. (Wages Commission n.d.: 20.) Second, the homelands' bureaux initiate the primary classification system. Thus the 'Tribal Labour Office' is given the responsibility of classifying every 'workseeker' into one of seventeen categories of employment – for example, 'agriculture', 'mining', 'domestic', 'construction' or even 'unemployable'. Registration as a 'workseeker' is compulsory for all adult males over the age of 15, but in a classic demonstration of Orwellian logic, workseekers are not allowed to seek work: they have to wait their turn at the tribal labour bureaux. (Regulation 21 of 1968.)

This primary segmentation of the labour force is then reinforced by three further control measures. First, a contract, without which a workseeker cannot take up employment. Needless to say, the employee is given no opportunity to negotiate the terms of the contract, and is in no position to enforce its terms, even where the contract offers some modest protection for the worker. Characteristically, the terms of the contract are not known to the worker and compliance is assumed after a process of mass thumb-printing takes place. Second, the labour bureaux structure the occupational mix according to manpower demands by refusing to reclassify the workers'

50

categories of employment, unless they select 'farming' or 'mining', the two most unpopular categories. Third, the labour bureaux control the geographical destination by only registering the worker for particular zones, where labour-power happens to be in short supply. Again, changes of zone would only be made to the most unpopular area.

The system of labour regulation as described worked reasonably well until the 1970s, when a period of unrest – including riots, boycotts, strikes and other forms of worker resistance began to shake the structures of the apartheid system. The highlights of these protests included a rolling wave of strikes initiated by unorganised workers in 1973 (see Dekker et al. 1975; IIE 1975) and an uprising in Soweto, commencing in 1976 (Hirson 1979). The state moved rapidly to try to repair the damage to political stability and a number of on-going reforms were initiated at the constitutional level with accompanying changes to the structures of industrial relations and labour control. In particular, two major governmental Commissions were set up. Because the Commissions were established in the wake of unrest and with a public rhetoric announcing a reforming mood from the top, the extent of the change was frequently exaggerated. Often, the proposals simply sought to rationalise, consolidate and modernise existing state practices rather than provide a genuine alternative to them. In other cases, the Commissions simply recognised that they could do little to reverse the level of industrial or popular struggles and sought simply to channel them into acceptable directions.

The two Commissions that pertain to my present concern were the Wiehahn Commission, whose recommendations resulted in the Labour Relations Act of 1981, and the Riekert Commission, whose report was submitted in 1978. The Labour Relations Act permitted Africans to organise and join registered trade unions. Moreover, these unions could be multi-racial in character. The qualifying adjective 'registered' was important in that it subjected the union to a wide range of checks by inspectors – of a financial kind, but also aimed at ensuring that the registered unions steered well clear of political organisations and involvement, had no significant foreign links, and would not grant strike pay to workers illegally on strike. In the course of parliamentary discussions these checks and restrictions were applied to 'unregistered' unions as well with the additional stick that they would find it impossible to operate a 'check-off' system without ministerial approval (Cooper 1981). The new labour relations order can be seen as a recognition that, in the wake of the massive outbursts of industrial unrest, the state had no alternative but to accept the reality of unionisation, and, given this fact, it was better to talk to legally-sanctioned representatives who might be amenable to state control than to spontaneously generated leaderships, unknown to the Labour Inspectorate. Though the provisions of the new Act applied to all workers, migrant or Section Tenners, there is little doubt that the stabilised workers benefited more from the Act in that they were more likely to join and sustain trade unions.

The Riekert (1978) Commission reinforced the relatively privileged status of the stabilised urban population, but also extended and refined the system of labour control in a number of important directions. Not all the Commission's recommendations have resulted in current legislation, but the report is crucial in understanding the broad direction of change in the labour supply system, which provides one of the major pillars of the apartheid state. The report of the Commission represents one of the most sophisticated attempts to design a segmented labour market by state intervention and therefore merits close attention by those who would hope to change this deeply imbedded part of the current social order. On the question of the supply of manpower, the report (Riekert 1978: 24) states:

> The most important question is whether the right quantity of labour at the right *quality* will be available at the right *time* and the right *place* to satisfy the demand ... [its] availability is determined by the following factors (a) the optimal allocation of the available pool of artisan and technically skilled workers in accordance with demand conditions; (b) the *timely* training of an adequate number of workers ... (c) the horizontal and vertical mobility of labour. The horizontal and vertical mobility of labour is determined mainly by the following factors (a) statutory, administrative and traditional constraints, (b) the preferences of workers and employers, (c) wage differences and (d) the availability of housing. [Emphasis in original]

The systematic construction of this agenda prefigures systematic attention to each aspect in the report. The net result was to rationalise and harden existing boundaries between the different labour markets by reinforcing discretionary and statutory differences. White and Coloured workers in artisanal or supervisory positions would of course retain their existing rights to organisation and labour mobility (within the constraints, in the Coloured case, of having to live in a group area designated for them).

However, a new group was to enter these 'privileged' ranks (though of course at a lower level). Section Tenners would be given the right to join trade unions, more mobility in terms of influx control (for example, the right to move between zones), increased access to housing and also higher wages (Claasens et al. 1980: 34). The housing concession is of particular interest in that, as pointed out earlier, by strict apartheid doctrine no black could ever own property in a 'white area', as freehold ownership would recognise a permanent right of residence. The compromise effected in the wake of the Soweto riots was to permit 99-year leases, with an option to renew. This satisfied apartheid doctrine on the one hand, and the recognised need for labour stabilisation and African demands on the other. The ideology will have to be readjusted again in the aftermath of the 1985 disturbances, when further concessions on property rights were presaged and freehold rights promised.

While Riekert undoubtedly strengthened the position of Section 10 blacks, he separated their fate strongly from other categories of workers – migrants, foreign workers, commuters and unemployed workers. In each case, the Commission recommended improvements to the organisational and institutional structure that policed these areas. For example, far from recommending closure of the labour bureaux system, Riekert sought to argue that the South African system was fundamentally similar to the employment services provided in the UK, the USA and West Germany. It was true that 'the general image of local labour bureaux in the eyes of employers and workseekers is very poor for a number of reasons, including their link with: influx control, unpopular types of employers who cannot succeed in recruiting workers and workseekers who cannot find work for themselves, and staff who are not trained for this type of work' (Riekert 1978: 140–143, 144). On the other hand, these faults were not intrinsic. Staff had to be better trained, private employment offices should also be permitted to offer their services under the control of the Department of Labour and separate service points should be established for professional, clerical and unskilled workers. In one area the Commission proposed a fundamental change, namely that workseekers should not be obliged to register at the bureaux (this placed men in the same status as women). However, Riekert (1978: 144) was in no doubt as to the continued relevance of the bureaux:

> A programme of action should be initiated to ensure the efficient functioning of the labour bureaux system . . . because it fulfills an important role in connection with the orderly canalisation of labour and the supply of labour in accordance with the demand for it.

As with the more efficient functioning of the labour bureaux, so the report also tidied up other 'anomalies'. For example, three of South Africa's major industrial areas are located in Pretoria, Durban and East London, cities also close to the existing 'bantustans'. Many workers from KwaZulu, Bophuthatswana and the Ciskei therefore tried to acquire Section 10 rights while commuting across these rather nominal boundaries. Riekert puts a stop to this by ruling that commuters should not be able to qualify for Section 10 rights. He equally rationalises the inter-state treaties (similar to the post-war West German treaties) regulating the supply of labour from foreign African states. Finally, his report contains some forceful recommendations designed to cut down the extent of 'illegality'.

In essence, the South African system of labour regulation is one that polices the external frontiers through immigration checks and inter-state foreign labour contracts, and polices internal frontiers (between racially-defined residential and industrial areas) through influx control. The particular feature that attracts such opprobrium to the South African system is that the state apparatus set up to enforce influx control uses particularly brutal methods. In addition, in the past the state sought to use influx control measures as a means of turning the indigenous (and voteless) black population into a foreign population. The recognition by the Riekert Commission that Section Tenners are in effect irremovable has stabilised and often significantly improved the conditions of life of the longstanding black urban population, perhaps 10–15 per cent of the black population as a whole. For the majority of black workers, however, there is little point in relying on the benevolence of the apartheid state. For them, the only means for self-improvement lies in self-organisation and protest.

Labour Protest

Restrictions of space prevent anything but the most abbreviated account of recent labour organisation and unrest. During the 1950s and 1960s, the state and the employers had become so relaxed in their labour market and work-place supremacy that the wave of strikes by 13,500 contract workers in Namibia in January 1972, against the pass laws and the humiliating conditions of the compounds, caught the employers and authorities by surprise. Just one year later, the secondary industries around the Durban-Pinetown-Hammarsdale complex erupted. Some 60,000 workers were involved in a set of protracted disputes. Parallel events on the Rand involved the bus companies, the clothing industry, newspaper and milk delivery services and engineering concerns. Although the mines were not involved directly in the 1972–3 events, they benefited from the conflict in that the scale of disruption indicated that black workers were not prepared to tolerate deteriorating living standards and the lack of representation at work. The strikes of 1972–3 were an important psychological as well as practical victory in that the sense of the employers' invincibility was shaken. A few years later, in 1976, the schoolchildren of Soweto provided another decisive challenge to white supremacy. Again, the miners were not involved; the authorities even attempted to use them against the urban rioters. But again the arguments for black representation were raised and answered on the streets. One of the young men who gained his political initiation in the Soweto uprising was Cyril Ramaphosa, later the principal organiser of the National Union of Mineworkers.

The awakening of the miners from their long slumber was seen in the late 1970s and early 1980s. At first, the stories of unrest were small items in the South African press, involving acts of looting, fighting, sabotage and fire-raising. Gradually some perceptive observers and journalists realised that the 'troubles on the mines' were much more extensive than the Chamber of Mines or the companies had admitted. One report claimed that during 1982 there were 'at least 70,000 men on strike. It was the largest action to hit the mining industry since 1946' (*Golden City Press* 12 September 1982). Thirteen mines were stopped, in one by 120 black miners sealing themselves in a tunnel.

The Chamber of Mines quietly conceded a number of wage claims, such that the average money earnings of Africans on the mines moved from 5.47 per cent of white earnings in 1972, to 17.79 per cent of white earnings a decade later (MacShane 1984: 51). They tried also to foster a compliant 'yellow union', but were forced by the strength of its organisation to recognise the National Union of Mineworkers, led by Ramaphosa in mid-1983. Ramaphosa capitalised on the high levels of militancy amongst African miners and, using the sympathies of the team leaders, was able within two years to boast the largest black union in the country. Legal strikes in September 1984 led by the NUM were followed in November 1984 by boycotts of taxis, sports events, liquor outlets and concession stores.

These struggles moved to a climax in April 1985 when 17,000 workers were dismissed in the western Transvaal, 13,337 from Vaal Reefs, the biggest mine in South Africa. Workers were bussed back to the homelands and to neighbouring states after a protracted tussle with the mine's security force. Ultimately the company, Anglo-American, agreed to take back the overwhelming majority of its dismissed workers, a course of action that would have been inconceivable a decade earlier. Anglo-American also took the lead in trying to settle the mid-1985 demand for an across-the-board 22 per cent wage increase. The Afrikaner-controlled company General Mining Corporation and some other mines where the union was weak, decided to slug it out, and precipitated a two-day strike (supported on the first day by 28,000 miners) in early September 1985. The usual pattern of dismissals and eviction from the hostels followed, though this time the union has taken the companies to court to prevent such conduct. By splitting the Chamber of Mines, forcing a favourable settlement in the mines where it was strong and showing its teeth even where it was weak, the NUM has made a decisive intervention into the state of national industrial relations. The exclusive white privilege of the blaster's certificate will soon be phased out, and further organisational advances and successful legal challenges are expected.

CONCLUSION: IDEOLOGY, CAPITAL AND THE LABOUR SUPPLY

As suggested in Chapter 1, one of the functions of all ideologies designed to secure legitimation for capitalist regimes is to suggest that the special interests of capital are coincident with the general interests of the population. I also pointed out, following Habermas, that in modern capitalist societies in Europe and the US, ideologies claim a technical and scientific character, seeking to use these claims to still keep power relations inaccessible and away from public analysis and criticism.

In these respects the apartheid theorists have attempted to perform the same sleight of hand, moving away from explicit racist declarations of *baaskap* (white control) to one which suggests that the organising principles of South African society are predicated on a technical appreciation of what is necessary in order to secure the efficient operation of society and the economy. Such a view can be seen in a speech by President Botha on 15 August 1985, where he claimed:

> We are not prepared to accept the antiquated, simplistic and racist approach that South Africa consists of a White minority and a Black majority. We cannot ignore the fact that this country is a multicultural society – a country of minorities, White minorities as well as Black minorities ... We believe in and uphold the principle of economic interdependence of the population groups, and accept the need for properly planned utilisation of manpower. In this regard we have advanced very far by modernising our labour laws.

The Riekert Commission is also replete with many comments of a technocratic character, perhaps best summarised in the report in some of the Commission's own 'points of departure', which are listed (Riekert 1978: 2) below:

> All undated or unnecessary statutory provisions as well as administrative rules in relation to manpower should be repealed.
> All inconsistencies in existing legislation, regulations and administrative rules that have a direct or indirect bearing on the utilisation of manpower should be eliminated.
> The procedures in connection with the administration of legislation relating to the utilisation of manpower should be simplified and streamlined.
> The effective functioning of the free labour market mechanism should be the object to be achieved by, among other things, strategic direct and indirect Government intervention with a view to the elimination of existing market failures, and by non-intervention where labour market results cannot be significantly improved.

Any recommendations arising from its terms of reference should be feasible and economically meaningful.

The political factors underlying the legislation to which the Commission's terms of reference relate, fall outside the scope of the Commission's inquiry.

Botha's speech and Riekert's recommendations are designed to show that the South African state stands above the particular interests of capital and above even the interests of the white electorate. This type of posture is one found in all states in that it provides a veil of legitimacy and secures passive assent, if not active agreement, to government policies. The difficulty with using apartheid in this role in South Africa is that it is all too clearly an ideology constructed initially and primarily in the interests of white supremacy. Although there have been many cosmetic changes and, indeed, substantive changes to the ideology, it still remains somewhat obvious as a veil, and does not clearly manage the *common* interests of capital.

For a while, it was the different interests of the three main branches of capital themselves – farming, mining and manufacturing – which permitted the apartheid state apparently to stand above the particular interests of each of these branches. In the case of farming capital, as we have seen, there was no initial contradiction between the white farmers and apartheid theorists: the main antagonism expressed was with mining capital which competed for the same cheap labour. In the case of mining capital, there were always some grounds for conflict, particularly over the question of family housing on the mines and the importation of large numbers of foreign migrants who threatened, if they 'leaked into the system' as illegals, to further tilt the demographic balance against the white population. Against this, there was a later coincidence of interests between the mines' need to internalise their supplies of migrant labour supply and the construction of the first bantustans which need to export labour-power in order to even appear as viable possibilities to their advocates. It was only in the case of manufacturing capital that the conflict between the need for a higher-waged, established proletariat and apartheid theory arose from the beginning. Though each section of capital had distinctive interests, as surmised by general theory, each sought to represent its special interests as the national good.

Farmers tried to represent their own interests as of national importance by appealing to the rural tradition of the Afrikaners, the alien character of urban capital and the need to develop export markets for wool, fruit and maize. Mining capital, for its part, could point to the high share of the gross national product that it accounted for, and the fact that gold represented a very secure hedge against world recessionary pressures. Even when a downturn of trade

57

occurred and the export market collapsed, more often than not gold or diamond shares would go up and provide an attractive bait to foreign investors. Mining therefore provided an insurance against good times or bad. A large company like Anglo-American, which controls 80 to 85 per cent of the world's diamond production and over one third of the South African gold mines, including the largest and the richest, could legitimately argue that what was good for Anglo was good for South Africa.

By the mid-1960s the group had also moved strongly into both finance and industry (Innes 1984: 188–228), thus blurring its specific sectional concern for mining alone. Anglo thus felt its interests move into harmony with those of manufacturing capital as well as the retail and commercial sector which needed a well-paid urban population to fuel a consumer market. This new coalition of capital financed a political party (the Progressive, later the Progressive Federal Party) and is represented in Parliament, though not in any significant numbers. There is no doubt, however, that with the rise of recent black protest, first in 1976 and again and more persistently in 1985, this coalition of mining, manufacturing and commercial capital now represents a more powerful force than its parliamentary numbers alone would imply. On the whole, foreign investors are linked to these elements of capital and even the farmers, for so long an unquestioning ally of the government, are seeing some advantage in pressing for larger shares of their produce being sold to a black consumer market. One illustration of this tendency was the lobby set up by Stellenbosch wine farmers to abolish the rigorous drinking laws preventing blacks from having free access to wine and spirits. The government is therefore poised uncomfortably between a fearful white electorate and a crudely reactionary political movement on the one hand, and the increasing stridency of black protest, implicitly supported by progressive sections of capital and international investors on the other.

The ways in which the apartheid theorists have sought to adapt to this dilemma is to try rationally to allocate the supply of labour fairly between each broad section of capital and to permit for the first time the growth of a propertied urban population. As to the continuance of the migrant labour system which remains at the heart of the allocation of labour, there is no doubt that this will quantitatively, but slowly, diminish. Botha has already made an explicit threat to the neighbouring southern African countries to the effect that their labour-power would no longer be required in South Africa should foreign sanctions have further effects. Although an ingenuous attempt to turn a tendency to rely on foreign labour less and less into a virtue and a bargaining card, the threat is probably an empty one. In a recent propaganda booklet called *South Africa: Mainstay of Southern Africa* (SAG 1985: 5) the Ministry of Foreign Affairs argued in this way:

The benefits accruing to the neighbouring countries go far beyond quantifiable earnings and contributions to gross national product. Employment of both *legal* and *illegal* workers in South Africa relieves the pressure on their labour markets to an enormous extent. This in turn promotes social and political stability in the countries concerned . . . If employment opportunities were to be reduced further by extraneous forces, such as sanctions, the Government would be obliged to give preference to the needs of its own citizens in the labour market. This would not be 'retaliation', as has been alleged. After all, charity begins at home, even in international exchanges. Imagine the effect on the fragile socio-economic fabric of the neighbouring countries if all these workers were no longer able to find employment in South Africa, or if the Government were obliged by circumstances to repatriate *illegal* workers on a larger scale. [Emphasis in original]

This threat to the livelihood of neighbouring countries is one that the South African government frequently deploys in moments of crisis, but their particular threat to foreign labour has the additional advantage that the government can appear to be safeguarding the interests of internal black labour ('internal' in this case also including the 'independent' homelands). Specious arguments of this kind have thus deployed apartheid theory to represent the sectional interests of the National Party and of the white electorate it serves, as the broader interest of the country. Nonetheless, this particular bit of bluster by the Department of Foreign Affairs is obviously not very convincing, particularly since South Africa's dependence on foreign labour is dropping as figures cited earlier testify. Instead, such a threat should be interpreted as Botha seeking to challenge the legitimacy of the powerful branches of capital – who in turn are being forced into an alliance by the pressure of black and brown protest. Claims as to who represents the national interest are now a matter for fierce ideological and practical contention between the state and capital.

4 Maintaining Social Control

In trying to examine the varieties of social control practised in South Africa, it is useful initially to make a brief allusion to Althusser's (1971: 141) distinction between what he sees as two kinds of state apparatus: '. . . the state apparatuses function both by repression and by ideology, with the difference that the repressive state apparatus functions incisively and predominantly by repression, whereas the ideological state apparatus functions massively and predominantly by ideology.' The first kind of apparatus depends on the overt use of force and violence by agents employed by the state such as the army, the police force or the secret services. The second refers to the more indirect means of control through 'the churches, schools, universities, trade unions, political parties' (Callinicos 1976: 74). This distinction has gained a great deal of discussion in left-wing writings insofar as it challenges the crude base/superstructure dichotomy of pristine marxism, and suggests that ideology and the state interpenetrate 'civil society' in a more complex way by securing the conditions of continued reproduction of the overall system. The distinction also operates on a more obvious level, raising the distinction between 'power' and 'authority' that has been a commonplace observation by political theorists since Machiavelli (1950: 32, 67) wrote of his *Prince* in 1513:

> It cannot be called virtue to kill one's fellow-citizens, betray one's friends, be without faith, without pity and without religion; by these methods one may indeed gain power, but not glory . . . with regard to the subjects, the prince may guard himself well by avoiding hatred and contempt and keeping the people satisfied with him, which it is necessary to accomplish . . . one of the most potent remedies that a prince has against conspiracies is that of not being hated by the mass of the people.

In South Africa as elsewhere, the phrase 'repressive state apparatus' captures well the deployment by the state of its near-monopoly of the organised means of violence in trying to enforce its will. However, Althusser's examples of the 'ideological' are unconvincing – in that 'churches, political parties and trade unions' are not particularly clear examples of 'state' institutions (at least in most capitalist societies), except in the most arcane use of that word. Pointing to such organisations also does not adequately depict the more informal means of securing consensus, through private agencies like the newpapers or advertising agencies, through state-supported services like health care, education, housing provision or recreational outlets, or through more diffuse processes such as accepted customs, norms, expectations, etc. I therefore consider it better to use more conventional sociological language and talk of the 'processes of socialisation' when looking at the means to secure ideological hegemony, popular support or, at the least, compliance by the populace. It is important to consider the latter, as most commentary on South Africa focuses on the more newsworthy repressive apparatus, rather than on how the state attempts to ensure compliance through other means.

Before commenting on these two elements of state power in the context of South Africa, it is important to add a third intermediate category to the modified Althusserian dichotomy. I refer principally to what Weber called the 'steel-hard cage' of modern bureaucratic systems (Weber 1968: vol.1) which intervene in all societies between the repressive fist of the state and its velvet glove. This tier of social control can be designated for the sake of convenience as the 'bureaucratic state apparatus'. Within South Africa, the major forms of bureaucratic intervention include the labour bureaux (discussed in Chapter 3), the bureaucracy directed by the Ministry of Co-operation and Development, the Department of Manpower and the various Administration Boards and Municipal Non-European Departments that direct the affairs of the urban townships. This 'steel-hard cage' traps the bulk of black and brown South Africans in a bewildering set of institutional arrangements, laws, regulations and conventions, typically symbolised in the 'reference book' which is carried by all black South Africans.

In the sections that follow I will look at the issue of urban social control in three respects: one, the operation of the military, police and National Intelligence Service; two, the bureaucratic state apparatus and the way in which it bears on the lives of urban black and brown South Africans; and three, the processes of socialisation, particularly in respect of housing, education, health and recreation. As some limitations of space inhibit the last section, I shall have to deal with it more cursorily.

THE REPRESSIVE STATE APPARATUS

It is almost self-evident to state that the implementation of enforced spatial segregation (described in Chapter 2) and the minute regulation of the labour supply (described in Chapter 3) require an effective state apparatus – a well-trained and well-equipped army and police force, a bureaucracy able to function without undue inefficiency and corruption, and a court and prison service able to process defaulters with dispatch and competence. The South African state has all these elements at its disposal, but it is worth remarking how recently these elements have been acquired, and pointing to some limitations of the repressive state apparatus.

At the turn of the century, the fathers and grandfathers of many of those supporting the most authoritarian features of the post-1948 state were in revolt against the British crown. The Boer War was fought with bitterness and determination by autarchic and highly democratically-organised *kommandos* (*ad hoc* military units). *Kommando* members were basically self-armed farmers acting in defence of their property and what they perceived as their interests or threats to their liberty. All members offered advice in Councils of War, acted on their own initiative, often used their own ox-wagons and family members and retainers as supply points, and obeyed a General voluntarily and only as a matter of personal respect. As Frankel (1984: 24) notes, 'the *kommando* was naturally antithetical to the development of the Boer into a distinctively professional and regular soldier'.

After the end of the Boer War, there were still many Afrikaners of a rebellious spirit who refused to accept defeat and who were known in the parlance of the time as 'bitter-enders'. Some went off to far parts, others stayed to fight another day. Their chance for revenge occurred both at the beginning of the First World War and at the beginning of the Second – when dissenting Afrikaner elements in the army sought to effect a political link with those Members of Parliament who were ready to join the German side. In both cases, the desertion of the South African side from the British Empire and Commonwealth was narrowly averted, but substantial numbers of disaffected military personnel and party supporters openly or secretly joined organisations like the *Ossewa Brandwag*, a quasi-military organisation in support of the Nazi cause.

This heritage of dissent and military rebellion has lent a special and rather sinister quality to the civil/military relation in South Africa. Fundamentally, there is no clear distinction between the two systems of power, even though the implantation of British institutions in the period after 1902 did promote a theoretical commitment to their separation. The divide between civil and military power breaks down, as Frankel (1984) argues, in two respects. Firstly, at the level of tactics – where the British model emphasises ultimate civilian responsibility for warfare by deploying disciplined troops, heavy fire power and military-style formations. The *kommando* inheritance, by contrast, emphasises the use of small, lightly-armed, highly-mobile units, geared to irregular and individual action appropriate to the conditions of a frontier society. The officer on the spot is the decisive actor. Secondly, the British tradition insists on a strong wall of insulation between the soldier and the politician, whereas the *kommando* tradition integrates the soldier into the mainstream of politics – where he becomes the disseminator of national ideologies, the protector of the cultural and moral instincts of the *volk* and the ultimate check on the politician.

Reference to the *kommando* tradition makes it possible to explain how, under the impact of urban unrest and guerrilla warfare, the Defence Force was able to transcend the 'moral barrier' between civilian and military society without internal conflict. The psychological fears that many whites feel, or are induced to feel, are also highly conducive to the growth of a dominant military ethic. The rise in military expenditure is but one index of the political ascendency of the military, Table 4.1 listing the allocations in recent years.

Table 4.1 *Defence Expenditure, 1958–1983 (Selected Years)*

Financial year	Millions of Rands
1958/59	36
1962/63	129
1966/67	255
1970/71	329
1975/76	1,043
1978/79	1,759
1982/83	2,668
1985/86	4,274

Sources: Frankel, 1984: 72; Omond 1985: 129.

Naturally, much of this expenditure is destined for external defence, fighting the war in Namibia and Angola, and for other military adventures in the region. However, the increased military expenditure also reflects the increased influence of the military in gaining a larger and larger share of resources for suppressing internal dissent. As discussion of the military sector is destined for a companion UNESCO volume (Minty forthcoming), I do not propose to elaborate here on details of the South African military procurement and strengths. Suffice it to say that, under full mobilisation, more than 400,000 soldiers could be called up. South Africa's armament includes 250 centurion tanks, 1,200 infantry combat vehicles, 313 combat aircraft, and perhaps 100 helicopters (Omond 1985: 133).

The breakdown of the thin line between civilian and military matters is also demonstrated by the increased influence of the State Security Council, both constitutionally and in practice. Members of the Council include the State President himself, P. W. Botha, formerly the Minister of Defence from 1966 to 1980, and General Magnus Malan, the former Chief of the South African Defence Force, who was brought into the Cabinet as Minister of Defence in 1980. The State Security Council acts to advise the government on the formulation and implementation of policy and strategy in relation to national security. But its functions go far beyond the normal brief associated with such a committee. As Omond (1985: 134) writes, 'through a number of committees it co-ordinates other government departments throughout the country dealing with matters like constitutional affairs, the economy, the military and police, civil defence, community services and cultural activities'.

Whereas the State Security Council represents the modern technocratic form whereby the military penetrate civilian matters, the *kommando* tradition is still very much alive at the local level. This accounts partly for some of the grossly excessive reactions by local commanders to threats of riot and peaceful demonstrations. To the rollcall of events like 'Sharpeville' must now be added names like Cross Roads, Uitenhage, Aliwal North, Soweto and Mamelodi, in which local commanders lost their heads and fired on unarmed or stone-throwing crowds.

The insensitivity of the police and armed forces to the national and international political implications of their actions seems almost unbelievable to observers reading police statements during the midst of the 1985 riots and the collapse of international confidence in the economy. However, such attitudes and behaviour by the armed services are consistent with the historical acceptance of initiatives by local officers. A few quotes will give the flavour of police reactions to the current disturbances:

'We are cracking down. We will not allow 5,000 stupid students to disregard law and order in Soweto and South Africa'. (Brigadier Jan Coetze, Soweto Police Chief after 800 children, some as young as 7 years old, had been arrested after school boycotts – *Guardian* 24 August 1985.)
'In our operations, the South African Police and the South African Defence Force operate as one unit'. (Brigadier Jan Coetze after soldiers on horseback had, together with police, rounded up 400–500 youths who had commandeered six tourist buses to take them to a court case – *Guardian* 18 July 1985.)
'Police do from time to time make use of helicopters in riots. It is possible that teargas cannisters were fired from a helicopter, but we were not informed of such an incident.' (Anonymous police

spokesman after 13 people were killed and cannisters were dropped from a helicopter during a peaceful demonstration outside the Mamelodi Town Council offices – *Guardian* 23 November 1985.)

'Botha has said we can kill you like flies'. (An alleged comment by police in Graaf Reinet who later killed the informant's son – *Guardian* 24 August 1985.)

'In Athlone yesterday there were persistent incidents of stone-throwing at vehicles and trucks. There is no doubt that these violent rioters had to be discouraged from continuing their wanton destruction of property'. (Captain Jan Calitz of the Cape Town Police defending a police ambush which resulted in the death of two boys aged 12 and 16 – *Guardian* 17 October 1985.)

'5,000 Municipal black policemen will be trained in the next six months. South Africa will not surrender to fire-raising, stone-throwing mobs'. (Mr Chris Heunis, Minister of Constitutional Development and Planning, at a passing-out parade of black police – *Guardian* 7 November 1985.)

The police force in South Africa like the defence force, has also been given huge budgetary supplements over the last few years. In 1985–86, the police budget was R954.7 million, up from R796 million during 1984–85 which was, in turn, 41 per cent higher than the previous year (Omond 1985: 136). All South African police are armed with a variety of weapons. White South African policemen invariably carry revolvers strapped to their waists. Additional weapons available to the police include truncheons, *sjamboks* (whips), teargas, rubber bullets, shotguns and assault rifles (the R1 semi-automatic). Black policemen, who constitute perhaps half of the force, are characteristically armed in a much lighter way – normally with truncheons and assegais (metal-tipped spears). It is symbolically significant that the white police retain the right to use the *sjambok*. An anonymous white national serviceman, who served with a police unit on 'township duty', points out that these rhino-hide whips, used by the police, are perhaps their 'truest symbol ... [used] for herding humans, baiting and punishing them – the tool of a base and perverted shepherd ... I have seen policemen wielding them on trapped and cowering offenders with all their might' (*Guardian* 6 September 1985).

In the wave of recent urban unrest, the police force has become virtually indistinguishable from the army units. Joint command structures, the use of armoured vehicles like Saracens, and joint expeditions mark the fusing of these two arms of the repressive state apparatus. The police, of course, are concerned primarily with ordinary criminal activity, as the rates of robbery, robbery with violence, and murder are amongst the highest in the world. However, the powers of the police in respect of entering premises, attending public and private meetings and searching without warrant, are now very extensive and the duties of the police clearly extend well beyond merely enforcing the criminal law (which of course is itself saturated with political overtones), to punishing assumed violations of security and law and order.

The incidence of violence in South Africa involving the police has now reached almost pathological proportions. Police are easily provoked into drawing lethal weapons, their treatment of suspects and arrestees is frequently disgraceful and their use of unnecessary force in respect of minor offenders has become so common as to be considered normal conduct. The police themselves have been subject to counter-violence by political and criminal elements, some 32 policemen having died in 1983. In the same year, a total of 189 policemen were convicted of common assault, 40 of assault with intent to do grievous bodily harm, 14 of culpable homicide and 3 of murder (Omond 1985: 140). Obviously these convictions are simply the tip of an iceberg and do not reflect the large number of cases of unreported violence, initiated either by the police or by prison warders.

While the picture of police brutality is one familiar to all observers of the South African scene, the more politically compelling question relates to whether the exercise of police and army violence is helpful to the regime in intimidating the populace, or whether it has now reached such proportions as to become counterproductive. A hint of the latter possibility was contained, for example, in a personal message issued by Brigadier van der Westhuizen, the officer commanding the Eastern Province Command, which was issued to all army units in the Eastern Cape during August 1985. The message read: 'The time has come to re-establish law and order. As members of a disciplined, effective and respected security force, each individual's conduct must at all times be responsible and courteous. We are confident that we shall win. Our cause is just. Always act honourably. Be a soldier that [sic] commands respect. Have confidence in your training. Remember: Respect human dignity' (*Guardian* 9 September 1985). The problem with such a message is that the army units are invariably tainted with the barbarous reputation acquired by the South African police.

The fact that the defence force, as pointed out earlier, has only a limited degree of insulation from the wider political and social structures of the society has meant that they are unable to represent themselves as a neutral force coming in to maintain law and order 'as a last resort'. For most black and brown South Africans, the army and police force are mutually reinforcing symbols and instruments of white supremacy. The attempt to try to soften the image of the army was also seen in what was described as 'Operation Smile' in May 1985, when troops handed out pamphlets showing a smiling soldier above the disingenuously simple caption: 'I'm your friend. Friends help each other. Thanks for your help'. As well as being naive, such operations do not form part of a consistent or longstanding policy, but represent tactical and immediate postures by individual commanders. They are therefore perceived by township residents as self-evident 'tricks', which do not represent the true attitudes of army and police officers.

A question related to the issue of police and army violence concerns the role of black policemen, nearly 17,000 out of 45,600 members of the police force in 1984. This is of especial salience in view of the expected white manpower shortages in operating the machinery of law and order. While nearly all white males are trained army reservists who can be called out to guard power stations, bus depots, airports and other strategic installations, there are ideological and practical limits beyond which the white army reservists will not be used by the regime. The practical limits relate to whether the loss of such manpower from its normal responsibilities will trigger bottlenecks in the economy and a further loss of confidence from foreign investors and governments. The ideological limits relate to whether the whites' acceptance of the regime can be ensured if 'the going gets tough'.

While for many Afrikaner citizens the devotion to such duties would be regarded as part of their wider responsibilities to the survival of the *volk*, for many English-speaking South Africans, together with recent white immigrants, their level of ideological commitment to the state is much more circumscribed. Indeed, one might argue that they stay in South Africa because of the easy, secure and affluent life style that it historically provided: it is doubtful whether their roots are sufficiently deep to sacrifice life or property for the maintenance of permanent white supremacy.

The use of black policemen therefore becomes an indispensable and growing part of South African strategy for urban social control. This potentially provides one of the most potent Achille's heels for the regime. Though it is easy for many township residents and exile organisations to denounce African policemen as 'stooges', 'Uncle Toms' or 'collaborators', in fact the political consciousness of black policemen is likely to be far more double-edged than these epithets suggest. There is little research evidence to cite in support of this last assertion but, as an illustration, I would like to mention the case of Sergeant Mohapeloa, a 48-year old policeman who had served for 28 years in the townships east of Johannesburg. His house was burned down in June 1985 by a crowd that broke the windows with rocks and hammers, doused the rooms with petrol and set them on fire. Despite his natural distress at this event, he too is clearly conscious of the fact that he is a victim of segregated facilities within the police units and the recipient of poorer pay. (Technically, the police force pays equal wages to black and white. However, inequality is ensured by promotion prospects. In late 1985, there were 14 black majors against 470 whites and 55 black lieutenants compared to 1,085 whites in the same rank.) According to Mohapeloa's interviewer, he feels the indignities of apartheid just as strongly as those who burned him out: 'I get angry just like them. I suffer just like them, I am paying rent just like them. I haven't even got a toilet' (*Guardian* 5 August 1985). Such an attitude, if representative, suggests that the white state will increasingly have to placate the views of black enforcement officers.

In some respects this scenario has been played out before – in three other historical events which bear some comparison to the current situation in south Africa. In the case of the American civil war, Lincoln was forced to rely on black troops defecting from the south or recruited in the north. His anti-slavery declaration can thus be interpreted as evidence of goodwill or moral generosity (the conventional view), but it can also be viewed as a pay-off to the black soldier. Again, in the First World War, while black troops died and fought next to their white comrades in arms, the concept of 'relative deprivation' was born in sociological language and a boost was given to civil rights and other movements for equal opportunities in the US. Finally, one can mention the case of the black troops recruited in the Second World War to defend the British and French Empires. There is no doubt that the pace of African, Asian and Caribbean nationalism was considerably advanced by returnee black soldiers as numerous accounts of the growth of nationalism in these areas testify.

The increased reliance that the South African state will be forced to place in the hands of black policemen also will mean that such officers will not accept being the unarmed or lightly-armed victims of crowd violence. They will demand, and the South African state will be forced to accede to their demand, proper weapons of self-defence – weapons that can ultimately be turned on the white members of the police force and army.

The most notorious agencies of social control in the South African repressive state apparatus are those concerned with internal security, particularly the Special Branch attached to the South African Police and the National Intelligence Service, previously known as BOSS (Bureau of State Security). The 1983–84 budget included a provision for a R796 million budget for the Security Branch and some R92 million (an increase of 25 per cent) for the other secret services.

The security forces have been exposed in numerous pamphlets and publications of anti-apartheid organisations as operating in a manner designed to intimidate, torture or, in some cases kill, opponents of the regime. Such pamphlets tell of detainees being pushed out of windows, held in solitary confinement for periods in excess even of the draconian laws and other general abuses of power. Yet one does not have to take the evidence provided by such organisations as the sole authoritative source, as members of the apartheid regime, in frequent lapses, often provide the same general indications. General van den Bergh, the former head of BOSS, for example, told a government Commission of Inquiry: 'I have enough men to murder if I said "kill". I don't care who the victim is. That is the kind of men I have' (*Guardian* 29 February 1985).

The operations of the National Intelligence Service also extend beyond the South African borders. From the mid 1970s on, in particular, the secret services of the state began to assume a much more offensive stance in view of the success of anti-apartheid campaigning in Europe, North America and African countries. Recent activities of this agency include: the attempt to discredit Jeremy Thorpe, the British Liberal leader, in connection with allegations of a conspiracy to murder his alleged homosexual lover; the attempt to frame Peter Hain, the anti-apartheid campaigner in Britain as a bank robber; the attempt to stage a coup in the Seychelles; and the probable involvement in the murder of Ruth First and other prominent leaders of the African liberation movements residing in Mozambique, Zimbabwe, Botswana, Swaziland and Zambia.

While the activities of the National Intelligence Service might be thought to be no less reprehensible than the operations of equivalent agencies like the CIA, the KGB or MI5, it is necessary to refer again to my opening comments concerning the very narrow boundary between civil and military relations which pertain in South Africa. The security services are closely identified with the Afrikaner nationalist cause and are predominantly staffed by Afrikaners whose career and promotion prospects depend on governmental favours. Of course, the National Intelligence Service does recruit agents, informers and *agents provocateurs* from other ethnic groups. For example, an English-speaking agent, Craig Williamson, was used to penetrate the offices of the World University Service in Geneva to provide information on students on its grants. Numerous black and brown informants are also paid to report on union and political meetings and the attitudes of members of civil rights, church and other anti-apartheid organisations. It is difficult to assess qualitatively the contribution of such agents to social control, though it is probably true to say that they were particularly effective in the 1960s when strong opponents of the government were unused to the idea of clandestine political organisation (having just emerged from a relatively liberal political order).

Now, many of the organisations opposing apartheid are better informed, are organised on cell lines and are sufficiently powerful to ignore the odd informer in their ranks.

THE BUREAUCRATIC STATE APPARATUS AND URBAN SOCIAL CONTROL

Between the obvious and powerful systems of violent enforcement of the state's will on the one hand and the more diffuse sources of ideological compliance lie the intermediate interventions of urban planners, statisticians, health boards, architects, social workers and the like. These elements constitute a technocratic group arguing for control and management systems of urban space that are politically neutral and depend for their adoption only on rational choice, or, in a utilitarian version, on 'the greatest good of the greatest number'. While modern conservative politicians, like Mrs Thatcher or President Reagan, often regard all forms of intervention by the state as 'soft liberalism', a number of influential reinterpretations of the United States' experience of governmental intervention in welfare issues have now produced a very different view of such actions. In examining the growth of relief and welfare systems in the US during the depression, Piven and Cloward (1971: 197), for example, point out that the motivation for introducing such measures did not stem from moral concern or 'soft liberalism':

> Mass unemployment alone did not lead to the expansion of relief arrangements – not, that is, until unemployment had generated so much unrest as to threaten political stability. In other words, economic convulsions which also produce mass turbulence – whether riots in the streets or upheavals in electoral alignments – are likely to lead to the temporary liberalization of relief provisions.

In another influential essay on the administration of welfare in the US entitled 'The Professional Bureaucracies: Benefit Systems as Influence Systems', the same authors (1972) show that the benefit systems installed by governmental intervention do not signify the irresponsible handing out of taxpayers' money (as modern monetarist theorists are wont to argue) but are in fact forms of control initiated by the state and amplified and set in place by the public and private bureaucracies that grow up around the administration of welfare. Piven and Cloward depict the case worker, guidance counsellor, educator, recreational expert or community organiser, whether working for a youth programme or something like Operation Headstart, as a professional agent for socialisation who defends and advances the propriety of middle class political values and the legitimacy of existing political arrangements. They continue (1972: 8):

> The low-income clientele whom the bureaucracies are charged to serve, to placate and to contain are a special source of sensitivity to them. Any disruption or assertiveness on the part of clients, to the extent that it is visible, will put in jeopardy the support of groups and organizations that watch over the public agencies. The bureaucracies therefore manipulate the benefits and services on which their clients come to depend in such a way as to control their behavior.

There are two arguments to be derived from this comparative case of the US, when applied to the context of South Africa. Firstly, it is apparent that the provision of a large volume of low-cost housing for black South Africans reflected, not so much the beneficent concern of the white state for poor people, but the need to control squatter settlements and unregulated private housing, with all that such settlements implied in terms of the possibilities for political mobilisation. Secondly, though the systems of welfare relief and professional bureaucracies described by Piven and Cloward for the US are not anything like as advanced in South Africa as they are in the United States, many examples of the same impulse for agencies to act or to be used as agencies of social control are now becoming more apparent. More often than not these agencies are tied to the apron strings of progressive capital (just as in the United States, the Ford and Rockefeller Foundations took leading roles in urban renewal programmes).

In 1953, the late Sir Ernest Oppenheimer, head of Anglo-American, provided the first major loan for the housing of black people. After the Soweto riots of 1976, representative bodies of commerce and industry in the Transvaal produced memoranda arguing for the improvement of legal and economic security of township residents, an amelioration of influx control, more and better housing with land ownership rights, wages and job opportunities, and the development of a black middle class. Charitable foundations such as the Urban Foundation emerged as a permanent institutionalised response to further these objects.

The Urban Foundation provides an interesting example of a growing unity between English-speaking and Afrikaner capital in that the leading lights of the Foundation were Harry Oppenheimer of Anglo-American who subscribed 34 per cent of the R32 million of operating funds (in 1981) and Anton Rupert, the Afrikaner tobacco giant. All the main South African banks and companies were involved (with the notable exception of Volkskas bank, which still distanced itself politically) and the Urban Foundation was able also to borrow R40 million from foreign banks, apparently equally interested in securing their investments through welfare provision. The Foundation's statement of objectives (cited Davies et al. 1984: 123) is explicit in arguing for the promotion of a black middle class with 'western-type materialist needs and ambitions'. Such a class is necessary, the statement continues, for:

> ... only by having this most responsible section of the urban black population on our side can the whites of South Africa be assured of containing on a long-term basis the irresponsible economic and political ambitions of those blacks who are influenced against their own interests from within and without our borders.

As this statement indicates, by 1976 business and commerce were taking a deliberately co-optionist path, against the wishes of the government, though, as Lodge (1983: 336) points out, the leading capitalists were still too timid to demand the logical supplement to a co-optionist path, namely a franchise for black and brown South Africans. Instead, the welfare and benefit systems put in place by manufacturing, commercial and mining capital sought to incorporate and stabilise the black population by all measures short of granting the possibility of direct political participation in the government.

The welfare providers set to work in townships like Soweto. With an official population of 864,000 and an unofficial population of perhaps one and a quarter million, Soweto was constructed virtually entirely without the normal urban facilities associated with a 'new town development' of this size and density. Nearly 105,000 dwelling units were built in Greater Soweto over the last forty years, and some indications of the extent of social, welfare, educational and recreational provision can be gauged by the data provided in Table 4.2.

Pitiful as some of these totals are, given the size of the population, they nonetheless indicate the modest success achieved, with the help of private foundations, in providing some welfare and recreation for Soweto residents. Considering also that the formal position of the government until 1978 (when 99-year leases were permitted) was that the population was simply there on a temporary migrant basis, the advances in urban welfare may be considered more striking. The original strategy of exclusion and the newer strategy of co-optation can be graphically portrayed by Levi-Strauss's binary opposition (cited Cohen 1985: 218–9) between 'vomiting out' and 'swallowing up' those who possess 'dangerous powers'. The option represented by progressive capital and the Urban Foundation comprises what Levi-Strauss calls 'cannibalism', absorbing those possessing dangerous powers as the only means to neutralise them. Pristine apartheid theory, on the other hand, can be considered the practice of 'anthropemy', ejecting dangerous members from the body politic and keeping them per-

Table 4.2   *Welfare Indicators for Greater Soweto, 1981*

Churches	303 + 900 sects
Schools	365
Nursery Schools and Creches	80
Trading Sites	1,700 (1,102 electrified)
Post Offices	4
Banks and Building Societies	8
Libraries	5
Beer Halls	7
Bottle Stores	12
Filling Stations	27
Amphitheatre	1 (12,500 seats)
Athletic tracks	4
Cinemas	4
Dance Halls	4
Cycling Tracks	1
Community Halls	6
Golf Courses	1
Cricket Pitches	6
Club Houses	20
Netball Fields	104
Stadiums	3
Soccer Fields	141
Park Areas	39
Hospital Admissions (Baragwanath)	117,917
Hospital Outpatients (Baragwanath)	390,131

Source: Official Figures, The West Rand Administration Board.

manently isolated. Though this physiological metaphor is used to analyse different strategies of deviancy control, it serves as well to depict the conflicting tensions within the current strategies of urban social control. As Cohen (*ibid.*) puts it, the swallowing-up mode stands for the possibility of incorporation, integration or assimilation; whereas the vomiting-out mode stands for the possibilities of separation, segregation, isolation, banishment and confinement.

Naturally, the two modes represented here are ideal-typical tendencies, one of which, the swallowing-up strategy, appears to be in the ascendancy. If we look at the way in which union organisations and movements for wider political representation were contained in Europe during the eighteenth and nineteenth century, we can see some broad analogies between the strategies used then and those now proposed by the leading sections of South African capital. Like the organised European workers, progressive capital wishes to provide a stake in the system and an inducement to defend that stake. Instead of only losing their chains, under the new scenario urban blacks will have a modest house, access to health, educational, welfare and recreational facilities, and a reasonably-paid job to lose in the event that they adopt a more revolutionary road.

As yet, it is unclear whether those that command the state will follow capital and move quickly enough in the direction of the swallowing-up mode to provide sufficient resources to create a stabilised black and brown urban group sufficiently committed to the *status quo*. For example, educational provision for the population groups is still dramatically different – during 1982/83, per capita spending on white school children was R1,385.00, on brown children R732.62 and on black children R115.19. Again, in the welfare budget for 1983/84, R469 million was spent on whites, R168.5 million on browns and R207 million on blacks in white areas. In respect of health provision, coverage can be indicated by the doctor/patient ratio – one for every 330 whites, 965 browns and 12,000 blacks (Omond 1985: 77, 68, 71). The disproportions of spending indicated in the three major welfare areas, and the increasingly powerful black and brown voices demanding equal treatment are together placing great strains on the public and private benefactors' purses – these demands coinciding, as they do, with falling profit levels, recessionary pressures and the likelihood of substantial and permanent foreign disinvestment. The swallowing-up strategy may therefore prove to be more like the 'biting off more than they can chew' option for government and capital.

I have already mentioned that one of the limitations to the control model supported by the private and public bureaucratic state apparatus is that (unlike in the United States) it operates without any direct rights of central representation by the clientele. In response to this deficiency, the state, contrary to apartheid orthodoxy, began to put into place a quasi-democratic local tier of government called the Community Councils. By the beginning of 1982, there were some 230 of these established under the 1977 Community Councils Act. However, by 1982, the Councils, according to Hughes and Grest (1983: 123 *et seq.*), had 'all but collapsed'. The views of the Councils were treated with contempt by the Administration Boards (which were the next tier of government and dominated by white administrators), the polls by which the councillors claimed election were farcically low, and their budgets were both miserly and allocated at the pleasure of the Department of Co-operation and Development – a ministry previously called the Department of Plural Affairs, previously called the Department of Bantu Affairs, previously called the Department of Native Affairs. The change in nomenclature did not alter the realities of centralised white power. Nonetheless, the bureaucratic state apparatus undergoes constant remodelling and retuning. A post-1983 refinement, for example, distinguishes between the 'hard services' (such as water, electricity, roads and waste disposal) which will be taken over by metropolitan boards (or left with the Provinces and Administration Boards), and 'soft services', such as parks, libraries and swimming baths which are specific to an area and also 'culturally sensitive'. Councils administering the soft services will also have limited rights to raise local revenues. The broad intention seems to be to place largely unrepresentative black councillors on the firing line to take the first shock waves of dissent, with the white administrators, holding the purse strings and controlling the bulk of the services, lurking quietly in the background.

THE PROCESSES OF SOCIALISATION

The final form of social control undertaken by the apartheid state comprises the non-violent and non-coercive, but nonetheless power-ful, attempts to influence the black and brown population in the direction of accepting the legitimacy of white rule. The ideological necessity for this exercise revolves around the gross incongruity between the small number of whites who rule or elect those that do, and the large number of blacks excluded from these possibilities. In this ideological form, apartheid supporters act to displace the major contradiction between white rulers and black ruled, by seeking to persuade the black and brown population that white is not only might, but also right. In this respect, apartheid represents a variety of elite theory (distinguished by intellect in Plato, royal birth in monarchies and 'race' in South Africa), the general principle being that only those 'fit to rule' should be entitled to do so.

The argument that blacks are not so entitled is reinforced by customs, norms, expectations and social practices that are informally conveyed in white attitudes and behaviour patterns, generationally transmitted by the family, the media and other social institutions. The notion that blacks are unfit to govern also rests on strong caricatures and stereotypes of the black and brown population. In everyday conversation, constant reference is made to other African countries where democracy is said to have failed or to have been exercised irres-ponsibly by those 'not fit to exercise a vote'. The fact that this notion denies the wisdom of devolving power to the homelands, as promoted by apartheid theory, does not trouble such critics of African pol-iticians. In white domestic households, male stewards and gardeners of whatever age are commonly referred to as 'the boy'; maids and female cooks are likewise referred to as 'the girl'. It is not uncommon to hear small white children mimic the white 'madam' and reprimand their nurse for some infraction of her duties, real or imagined.

Though there are obvious comic aspects to such absurd social conventions, they are also painfully insulting and perform the ideological function of reducing the black population to a pre-majority childlike state in their human development. Those blacks who behave submissively are rewarded with the dubiously generous appellation of a 'good boy', those who show pride or defiance are 'cheeky Kaffirs'. So ingrained have these forms of address and insult directed against the brown and black population now become, that many whites would not necessarily recognise them as a conscious means of inhibiting and subduing black demands for dignity and recogition.

In a popular song, Ray Charles sings that 'Sticks and stones may break my bones, but talk don't bother me'. To the extent that the subordinate groups in South Africa are resilient enough to ignore the indignities heaped upon them, they are immune from white hatred and ridicule. However, unlike the black singer, Fanon, in his powerful psychiatric studies of Algeria (1970), sees a wholly neurotic dialectic in the verbal and other interactions between the races in a colonised society. Through custom, language and lopsided forms of social conduct, the black man acquires the stigma of irremovable inferiority. His shame at being constantly 'dissected with white eyes' turns him in on himself to the point of self-hatred. So powerful is this attack on his psyche that he loses the ability to make choices and has to conceal his black skin behind a white mask. In later works, Fanon probed the therapeutic value of violence in seeking to escape this sense of shame and paralysis. Without going into the complex moral arguments that Fanon's views have provoked (for example, is violence by a subordinate group more defensible than violence by a superordinate group?), it is possible to see in the current spate of township violence some of Fanon's preoccupations being worked out. Blacks are recovering their dignity and humanity by exercising their power and expressing their defiance. How else are we to explain the almost contemptuous disregard for the army and police forces' firepower shown by youths picking up bottles and rocks to oppose carbines and armoured cars?

Of course, South Africa is not Algeria, and it is sometimes difficult for the outside observer to judge how much apparent compliance by some blacks and browns in the apartheid system actually constitutes the internalisation and acceptance of white-held stereotypes in the sense understood in Fanon's early writings, and, by contrast, how much is a form of dissimulation – with black and brown people acting out their assigned roles without conviction. The point is perhaps best made by referring to the case of 'Sambo', the bow-legged, southern US slave, who clowns and dances and rolls his eyes. When a black man in the US played Sambo, he played the role assigned to him by the white slaveowner, but he did so in so exaggerated a manner that, in effect, he provided a parody, critique and refutation of the stereotype. Similar complex interactions occur in social relations between the population groups in South Africa. Take, for example, the sight of a Coloured workman in a drunken stupor in the streets of Cape Town, enjoying the opportunity afforded by drunken licence to abuse the government, revile his boss or make lewd sexual innuendos to passing white women. Another commonly-observed sight is a black work-gang echoing the slave gangs of the American south by rhythmically chanting insults directed at their white overseer, who remains in blissful ignorance of the meaning of the words so cheerfully sung by 'his boys'.

Whereas the above two examples are of dissimulation without compliance, there are also no doubt cases, akin to Fanon's observations, of genuine internalisation of white hegemony by the subordinate classes. A social psychologist, Lambley (1980: 123), for instance, talks of some apparently masochistic black intellectuals, artists and professionals, who remain in the country 'because they need the situation to function properly'. According to his account, such individuals are able to institutionalise their victim status, without having to do anything about changing it. By being permanent victims, they can also escape responsibility for their acts and develop an inverted morality. In this case, apartheid becomes a functional system permitting psychological adjustment or even comfort.

In other cases, apartheid is not accepted as a psychological prop but deployed more cynically and more instrumentally to obtain favours. Lambley (1980:118–119) provides the following examples of such transactions he witnessed while living in a multi-racial pocket in Cape Town during the years 1967–70: (a) a white shopkeeper used to approach one of his Coloured shop assistants and threaten to fire her if she did not grant sexual favours; (b) a similar episode occurred with an illegally-resident black woman where the sanction would be greater and the woman was forced to comply or be threatened with the loss of her precarious position in the city; (c) a Malay shopkeeper was caught smoking marijuana in his backyard by a policeman. He was not charged in exchange for providing a regular supply of the drug to the policeman. In another case, known personally to this author, a brown woman who had 'passed for white' for a number of years was threatened with 'reclassification' unless she provided information to the security services. In all these cases the existence of an implacable racist state with powerful laws and sanctions is accepted by the social actors and manipulated by the more powerful against the less powerful. Occasionally, however, the boot can be on the other foot as in this case (witnessed by the author in a Johannesburg magistrates' court in the early 1960s) of a black maid who extorted money from her white employer, a minister of the Dutch Reformed Church, on threat of exposure of their illegal sexual relationship. In all cases of this kind, racism has itself turned into a commodity, which can be used, bought, sold or exchanged in the market place of ordinary transactions.

Black, brown and white attitudes and behaviour patterns are forged in this crucible of everyday interracial contact, but the strong caricatures and stereotypes of the 'Other' that emerge are also systematically orchestrated through the 'official' processes of socialisation. Let me take as a key example the images held of blacks by whites. These are much more diverse and mutually contradictory than may appear at first sight. I have already mentioned the possibility of being 'a good boy' or a 'cheeky Kaffir'. Blacks are also allowed to be 'good workers' but they cannot show 'initiative' (this sanction conveniently protects the white worker). They are 'violent','tribalist' and 'vengeful' (which justifies the state's control measures), though paradoxically 'good with babies' (which allows the employment of black nursemaids). These images are constructed, amplified and filtered by the state's socialisation processes. This is possible as the allocation of housing, access to health care, much of the media, and the educational system are either direct government services or provided by agencies or interests not prepared to oppose the government.

As I have mentioned, housing is consistently provided in a manner which is designed to suggest that blacks should not qualify for anything of better aesthetic appearance or design. The compounds and the townships were constructed essentially as temporary barracks, with minimal facilities. Often they were ringed with barbed wire giving the impression to the inhabitants and the passer-by that therein resided caged animals. The townships were vastly extended from the 1950s onwards to counteract the threat posed to the dreams of the apartheid theorists by private housing (which implied permanence) and squatter developments (which implied a lack of regulation of the labour supply). However, the level of demand for urban housing consistently and vastly outstripped government supply. Lea (1982: 200,205) takes the view that the post-Soweto reforms in housing tenure are largely a manifestation of the serious shortfall in provision during the 1970s when 'it appears likely that the government deliberately slowed down the rate at which houses for blacks were being constructed'. Similarly the extension of the 30-year leasehold to the 99-year leasehold, which was represented as a government-led reform, was probably due to pressure by the building societies for a greater security for their loans. The current strategy comprises a grudging recognition that the private market and self-help will have to make up the shortfall in government provision, but that only those with permanent urban rights will have the opportunity to benefit from such schemes. As Wilkinson (1983: 276) writes:

> For the state, the new strategy represents a potentially more sophisticated form of control of the urban African population. Tying the right to remain in urban areas to 'approved accom-

modation' and then setting in motion a 'free market' in African housing establishes an efficient basis to separate those potentially co-optable from marginal elements.

In the case of health provision, the historical gap between black and white provision has not narrowed significantly. TB, gastroenteritis, measles, and malnutrition continue to be the major killers of blacks. As long as these problems can be isolated to 'black space' (see Chapter 1), the medical services do not respond effectively. On the other hand, when cholera and bubonic plague were announced in 1982, diseases that could easily enter 'shared spaces', extensive inoculation took place. In the state's own health plan, there should be four hospital beds for every thousand patients. On this basis, there are 9,000 too many beds for whites and 17,000 too few for blacks (de Beer et al. 1983: 267). As in housing, and partly due to the current fiscal crisis, there has been a recent emphasis on self-help and private provision in health care, often dressed up in the language of 'community participation'. As a result, the state institutions, like Baragwanath hospital in Soweto, are starved of funds – a condition reflected in the extensive strike by nursing and para-medical black staff in 1985. Treatment routines in Baragwanath and on the mines are based on attendance to injury and short-term illness. Preventive medicine accounts for less than three per cent of the health budget, old and long-term patients often being ejected to find their way back to the bantustans. The inference we can draw from these data is that the underlying logic of health care for blacks is to patch up workers to return to their jobs, rather than provide a positive health programme for a permanent resident community.

Some brief words are necessary concerning the role of the media in trying to promote the ideological hegemony of apartheid. It is true that a number of the newspapers are privately owned and some show a healthy display of editorial independence within the constraints of the censoring laws and despite intimidation (though the most prominent of the liberal English-speaking papers, *The Rand Daily Mail*, was closed for commercial reasons in 1985). But the radio and television are strictly controlled by the government. Despite its wealth, South Africa only acquired a television service in 1976, a particularly backwoods Minister having delayed its introduction on the grounds that friends of the Minister who had visited Britain told him that 'one cannot see a programme which does not show black and white living together, where they are not continually propagating a mixture of the two races' (cited Omond 1985: 199). When television finally was introduced, two channels were reserved for own-language black programmes – a model previously followed in radio. A commonly-derived news service for all four channels is heavily saturated with government propaganda. So rigorous are the controls over separate language stations and channels that 'Soweto-language' and music (that is, shared, and often anglicised words or jazz sounds commonly used in the townships) are scanned out in favour of 'tribally-pure' language and music. As well as promoting apartheid, control over the media enables the government to censure news coverage of trouble-spots, a power enforced during the latter half of 1985. As a consequence, it is still possible for some white residents, insulated in their own territorial space, to imagine that the social movements of blacks are of no fundamental importance to their lives; they can live, truly, in a fool's paradise.

The final process of official socialisation I wish to comment on is the provision of education. Verwoerd set the prevailing tone in 1953 when defending the Bantu Education Act. He posed his vision (cited Neame 1962: 95) in this way:

> What is the use of subjecting a Native child to a curriculum which in the first instance is traditionally European? What is the use of teaching the Bantu child mathematics when it cannot use it in practice? That is quite absurd. Education must train and teach people in accordance with their opportunities in life according to the sphere in which they live.

In line with this policy, educational textbooks, designed for use in black schools, distinguished between civilised whites and uncivilised blacks while the syllabuses made clear that blacks were meant to imagine a life only of toil. Every black school, for example, was forced to have a period of gardening included in the curriculum. It was not until 1981 that a government-appointed Commission sought to shift the basis of education away from racial categories and more in the direction of the manpower needs of the economy. This followed years of complaints by manufacturing and mining capital of the 'skills shortage'. As Chisholm and Christie (1983: 258) comment:

> ... this emphasis on skill shortages is crucially important in negotiating a new 'common sense' about education. It makes obsolete the language of Bantu Education, and makes possible the ideological incorporation of sectors of the black population. 'Skill shortages' becomes a means through which consent to restructuring is won. Through .it, limited upward mobility, facilitated through the restructuring of the racial division of labour, comes to be seen as a possibility – if not a reality.

CONCLUDING REMARKS

One of the ideological functions of apartheid is to try to reconcile the huge disparities of power, wealth, opportunity, housing, health and educational provision as between whites on the one side and blacks and browns on the other. This ideological task is important to the whites, so that they can remain secure in their illusions that the government is doing all it can to help blacks and, where that is 'impossible', doing all that needs to be done to control any potential threat from the black and brown population. The lack of *angst* and guilt found in studies of the white population (one of which was cited in Chapter 1) is evidence that apartheid has generally been successful in convincing Afrikaners and many English-speaking whites that any further provision for black and brown citizens would be unnecessary and injurious to white interests.

However, apartheid has been less successful in subordinating independent black forms of consciousness. This is not to underestimate the powerful effects of the informal and official processes of socialisation discussed above, nor to ignore the 'iron-hard' cage of laws and regulations that inhibit group protest and action, nor again to forget the virtual monopoly of violence that is being used by the state to suppress dissent. What can be said more definitively is that, with the exception of some bantustan leaders, black and brown political demands have not followed the lines of apartheid orthodoxy. In other words, the ideological resistance by the subordinate population to the daily humiliations of life and the sustained official assault on their *weltanschauung* has not been successful. As well as physical resistance, the core of black and brown demands has remained, despite nearly forty years of apartheid, the institutionalisation of equal opportunities for all population groups in a unitary state. Whether such an outcome can be anticipated from the current wave of protest and unrest is a question addressed in my final chapter.

Conclusion: Apartheid is Dying but Will it Lie Down?

SOME CONSERVATIVE PREDICTIONS

As one might expect with so precarious and uncertain a situation in South Africa, there is no shortage of journalists, academic commentators, politicians and other observers who wish to act as seers predicting the future outcome of the current political and social changes in South Africa. Every leader writer on every newspaper from Afghanistan to Zimbabwe has had a say on the matter. It is impossible to give balanced coverage to the full variety of views, particularly since most of them are neither based on any close appreciation of South African history, nor written by professional social scientists sharing an agreed repertoire of concepts and methods. Rather than try to survey popular or international political opinion, I have decided to select three academic, and supposedly objective, views for especial attention. All three positions are what might be called 'conservative', in so far as they all cohere around a certain common stance – namely that the capacity for revolutionary change in South Africa is exaggerated, that the capacities for the regime to adapt are underestimated, and that it may be possible to contain dissent and unrest to a manageable level.

Of course, this consensus between the three views I summarise below is in one sense an artificial one, in that it could be assumed that I am prejudging by my selection the outcome of more contested arguments. This is to some degree true, though each viewpoint stands as a valid contribution in its own right judged purely on professional standards. The three authors also all attempt to grapple with what I judge to be the dominant dialectic of the endgame in South Africa, that between change and continuity, between evolutionary and revolutionary prospects. Later in this chapter, I provide a list of five of my own assumptions concerning a future South Africa, my own reading of the current situation pointing to a much more fundamental shift in the social order than any of the three conservative authors suggest. By summarising their views, at first without a critique, I hope to provide enough material to allow the reader to come to a more nuanced judgement of the balance of probabilities in the South African endgame.

A Pragmatic Race Oligarchy?

The first view covered is that provided in Adam's much discussed book, *Modernizing Racial Domination* (1971). Though the earliest of the three views, it is the most sophisticated, in that the author is fully cognisant of the repressive and unstable elements of the regime, yet nonetheless seeks to demonstrate how it has the capacity to develop a set of pragmatic policies in response to pressure. The regime is broadly characterised as a 'pragmatic race oligarchy', though the ideology of apartheid itself is thought to have certain utopian elements. According to Adam (p. 69), 'Verwoerd realized that he had to create a political outlet for African nationalism. The bantustan policy is supposed to fulfill this function. It deflects political aspirations to areas where they are no danger to white rule.' He suggests, quite plausibly, that the bantustan policy is not that different from the policy of indirect rule successfully practised by colonial administrators all over Africa. Adam surmises further that, in the short run, black 'satraps' will be satisfied with the minor privileges conferred by the apartheid state, given that their historical experience has comprised nothing but degradation and subjection (p. 80). However, Adam was convinced, as indeed subsequent developments show, that the homelands policy could only provide a minor solution to the problem posed by the growth of an urban African population. He also maintains that it is impossible to segment South Africa's economy, given the close interpenetration of white capital with black labour (cf. my own views in Chapter 1 above). He deals intermittently with the important question of rising expectations and the gap between 'claim' and 'reality', arguing, with good comparative support, that poverty alone is no guarantee of a heightened political consciousness. He opines that 'in South Africa an expanding economy has made it possible so far to meet the rising material expectations and not to heighten the discrepancy between ideology and reality' (pp. 101–2). In Adam's view, the main lever for pragmatic adaptation lies in the increasing heterogeneity of the Afrikaner population. With the poor white problem virtually solved or reduced to minor proportions, large numbers of Afrikaners are entering managerial, professional and business positions. These form the core of the *verligte* (enlightened) element, who will be able to propel their more traditional co-ethnics (the *verkrampte*) to compromise and adapt to new conditions. He sees apartheid as an 'elastic' race nationalism capable of internal liberalisation, in contrast to the irrationality of national socialism in Germany, and continues (pp. 181–82):

Above all, rational racial domination is most likely to falsify the assumption that mounting internal tension will make a violent revolutionary change inevitable. The South African whites, who at present determine the racial policies of their country, have almost perfected their domination over the non-white labor potential, and they will continue to do this in their own interests. They are not, as often viewed by the outside world, blindly fumbling toward their inevitable end. They are effective technocrats, who are establishing an increasingly unshakeable oligarchy in a society where the wealth of an advanced industrialization in the hands of the few whites coexists with the relative deprivation of the non-whites. If this is to be cemented by a gradual deracialization and economic concessions, South Africa's white élite is capable of achieving this in spite of internal contradictions.

A Multi-Ethnic Elite?

The second view I wish to cite was provided ten years later by Gann and Duignan in *Why South Africa Will Survive* (1981). Though claiming to be an independent historical analysis, the two authors are undoubtedly engaged in a polemic against what they see as a liberal and marxist orthodoxy regarding the South African government's wickedness and the country's potential instability. Their rebuttal of this perceived orthodoxy rests less on their training in historiography and more on their skills as polemicists. Instead of history, they provide a series of point-scoring propositions not far different from those usually emanating from the Department of Information in Pretoria. The broad drift of their argument is to suggest that the trickle-down effects of successful modernisation will dilute black claims, that the government is in large measure invincible and that despite, or because of, the possibility of violence killing the golden goose for all, the various ethnically-distinct élites will be able to cobble together a new and workable constitutional order. These arguments are developed in Gann and Duignan's final chapter (pp. 288–304) in the following, and similar, pronouncements:

> Unlike a truly decadent ruling class, South African whites are willing to tax themselves heavily and to conscript their sons . . .
> The whites perform essential economic functions; for the time being the greater part of South Africa's administrative, entrepreneurial and technical skills . . .
> South Africa – alone in sub-Saharan Africa – has built up a reasonably balanced economy complete with modern manufactures, extensive mining industries and an advanced agricultural sector.
> In military terms, South Africa is well equipped. It is a match for any conventional opponent except a superpower. South Africa is equally prepared to deal with guerrilla incursions.

84

. . . the benefits of economic development have begun to trickle
down to all racial groups, albeit in uneven measure. Black South
Africans – despite their disabilities – are among the best-paid,
best-educated, most urbanised blacks in Africa . . . UN propaganda notwithstanding, there are now substantial numbers of
black South Africans who have a great deal more to lose than
their chains.
South Africa . . . is not sufficiently dependent on imported
capital to be vulnerable to ultimata from the outside world.
Because conflict will not resolve the country's problems and
consensus may be impossible to achieve, a third way should be
tried – a consociational system . . . Consociation implies continued social and ethnic diversity based on a policy of
pragmatism and tempered by co-operation between the élites in
each social group.
Reform in South Africa will come from within. It will derive
from the ruling Nationalist Party rather than from a divided
opposition . . . The National Party today is a coalition . . . [with]
. . . a substantial reformist group made up of businessmen and
professional people, technicians and specialists in both the
public and private sectors, clergymen and senior members of the
defence establishment anxious to strengthen the country's industrial power and determined to create a wiser social consensus.

An Impasse?
Again without further commentary at this stage, I want to cite the third
and final view of the limited possibilities for fundamental change in
South Africa. It comes from an article by Schlemmer entitled
'Build-up to Revolution or Impasse?' (1983). The main thrust of his
analysis is that South Africa is far from being particularly unstable by
world standards. He argues that the source of most instability derives
from outside threats rather than internal dissent. He claims that a
series of survey research results demonstrate that blacks are adopting a
cautious political response, despite high levels of dissatisfaction,
because the instruments of coercion and control are too strong for
them to oppose. He adopts a modified version of Gurr's (1970) criteria
explaining 'why men rebel'. While survey evidence conducted in 1982
shows 'very high' and rapidly-increasing levels of expressed anger,
impatience and dissatisfaction (p. 67) and other indicators show a
'potential for political aggression or violence' (p. 72), he argues that
the minimum political demands by a wide cross-section of blacks are
surprisingly moderate. Schlemmer also reports that 70 per cent of
blacks surveyed in 1982 valued white participation in South African
society and white technical expertise, and that many saw the
possibility of patience, negotiation and the building up of bargaining
power leading to peaceful reforms and concessions (pp. 76–7). He

concludes by arguing that Gurr's structural and organisational criteria for 'turmoil', 'civil war' or effective 'conspiracy' are not met by black political leaders inside South Africa. Though he accepts that political discontent among the blacks is constrained by coercion and fear, Schlemmer goes further in assuming a more positive compliance by blacks derived from: (a) the incremental improvements in material welfare; (b) the opportunities for social mobility by educated blacks in the administrative system of the apartheid homelands; and (c) the creation of a more legitimate system of black local government. Short of high levels of externally-based insurgency, Schlemmer maintains that 'real or apparent system responsiveness, coupled with effective security controls and an emasculation of counter-system organisation, is likely to continue to protect the established regime functions, at least in the short term' (p. 79).

A MORE RADICAL SCENARIO: A CRITIQUE OF CONSERVATISM
AND FIVE ASSUMPTIONS

Adam is undoubtedly to be congratulated for uncovering, against the prevailing conventional wisdoms, the pragmatic possibilities that inhered in so apparently an implacable ideology as apartheid. At the same time, like the other authors I have grouped with him, he is essentially a 'top-down' theorist. They all find the final locus of power in the groups that wield it and insist on locating any movement in the system within the broad ruling group. Thus, Adam fixes on the *verligte* (the enlightened Afrikaner) to make his system more flexible and responsive; Gann and Duignan talk of a 'substantial reformist group' within the party; while Schlemmer (1983: 73) contents himself with saying that 'the degree of regime surveillance, control, action against radical organisations as well as its motivation (its white leadership and substantial white personnel ensures loyalty) is sufficient to discourage any organised attempts to confront the system.' Schlemmer (1983: 67) seems even to doubt that the regime has any real intention to promote reform – 'vague and sweeping promises of reform and development' are simply made from 'time to time' as a sop to world opinion.

By focusing only on the capacity of the regime to effect changes, we are given absolutely no sense of the degree of organisational capacity, political consciousness or level of mobilisation of the subject population. This same top-down blindness leads conservative theorists to believe the regime's own statements about itself – surely an unwise procedure for any social scientist examining any regime. This is less true of Adam, who does maintain a sceptical distance, but all too apparent in Gann and Duignan. Their statements that South Africa can 'deal with a guerilla incursion' and is 'not sufficiently dependent on foreign capital to be vulnerable to ultimata' have turned out to be empty, in that they do not square with the success of sabotage attacks and the collapse of the Rand in the face of a squeeze by foreign capital during the course of 1985. Schlemmer (1983: 73) displays a similar credulity about regime claims in quoting, and apparently accepting, police statements affirming that 'over ninety percent of underground insurgents who have participated in some act of sabotage are tracked down.'

Without labouring the point, it is clear that top-down analyses no longer work and that the continual challenges to the regime since September 1984 suggest a much more radical scenario than that imagined by the three conservative theorists quoted.

To make sense of the shifting ideology and practice of apartheid at this crucial conjuncture it is necessary to see how the government will have to react to pressures from the bottom of the social structure rather than from within its own ranks. To further this exercise, it is helpful to make certain assumptions about what the shape of a future South Africa might look like, in order best to identify those elements of a social structure that will remain unamenable or not easily amenable to political change, compared to those elements that will be subject to an almost immediate change should the current ruling class lose political power. I make five assumptions before undertaking this evaluation.

Continual Unrest

First, the incidence of urban unrest, the level of black political consciousness and the loss of confidence by foreign investors in the future of South African capitalism are not temporary phenomena. In the past, after Sharpeville and even after Soweto, urban unrest was damped down, investment trickled back and the regime appeared to regain its old trajectory. When the current wave of unrest began in late 1984, a number of commentators made comments of a rather similar kind, assuming, that is to say, that a few nervous whites would leave, the stock exchange would dip briefly, some more blacks would get shot, but that ultimately there would be a return to a stable equilibrium enforced by the awesome power of the apartheid state. However, a high and constant level of counter-violence directed against the state has continued, at the time of writing, for more than fifteen months, with no sign of it abating. Abroad, the campaign for divestment and disinvestment has taken grip of the young and radical elements in Europe and the US in a way that is only paralleled by the peace movement. Bankers appear ready to reschedule debts (for what else can they do?) but not to advance new loans. Even stalwart international investors like Barclays Bank, who were previously willing to subscribe to Defence Bonds, plan to reduce their participation in their local subsidiary to a minority shareholding and appear ready to criticise the regime openly. Virtually every day sees the announcement of some extension of the 'boycott South African goods' movement. These developments suggest that, far from drifting into the temporary doldrums of uncertainty, the apartheid ship of state has sailed permanently into an angry hurricane of protest.

An Unstable Equilibrium

Rather than assume a deviant situation returning to a stable equilibrium, it seems safer to affirm – and this is my second assumption – that what we are witnessing now are the beginnings of a new long-term unstable equilibrium, such as that obtaining in Northern Ireland or Lebanon. Obviously these analogies do not hold in any exact sense – they are simply meant to reinforce my second assumption that social and political relations in South Africa cannot be restored to the *status quo ante*. They are, on the contrary, likely to be constantly in flux and will probably retain a fair share of unfocused (and more directed) violence, urban disorder, mass struggle, state brutality and economic crisis.

Would these two assumptions, namely of a continuous challenge to the structures of apartheid and the development of an unstable equilibrium, alter dramatically if black rule is attained? One of the major difficulties in assessing such a proposition is that we are not certain whether, in a free competition for electoral advantage, a clear black and brown coalition would emerge. On the one hand, despite the apartheid state giving this movement more credence than perhaps it is due, there is little doubt that a black conservative party under the leadership of a figure like Chief Buthelezi would attract political support by a significant section of a black electorate. On the other hand, the representative organisations of the black and brown population that operated in the 1950s and were banned in the 1960s have existed largely only in exile for 20 years or more. These organisations are split amongst themselves, though it is clear that the African National Congress is the dominant force. The events of 1976 and of 1984/85 suggest that the historic role of the ANC has not been forgotten by current leaders of the black struggle. Many of the symbols and colours shown at black funerals and rallies are declarations of support for this dominant force of the liberation movement. The ANC has also acquired a reasonably strong presence on the ground through underground work in the communities, in the trade unions and through spectacular acts of sabotage.

However, the main effective internal coalition is the United Democratic Front (UDF) which in many respects continues the old traditions of front and alliance politics established by the ANC. It is, however, an organisation with its feet closer to the ground, is run by a younger leadership and has proved its worth in popular confrontations with the government. For many years, white supremacists have been so conditioned to seeing the exiled ANC as the embodiment of evil, a nest for communists and a harbinger of terrorism, that they have found it quite difficult to adjust to the fact that their internal opposition may represent a more potent threat. It is therefore quite likely that the ANC will go through a period of rehabilitation in the minds of progressive capital, liberal whites and, finally, government representatives. The game plan behind this refurbishment of the ANC's image will be to use the high prestige in which the ANC leadership is still held to quieten the more racist and more radical voices amongst the internal opposition. The speculation concerning Mandela's possible release is part of this wider calculation. For his part, Mandela is evidently wary of being used by the regime to 'cool out' the current wave of unrest and may think that he is a more potent political symbol behind bars than in front of them. Whether the other ANC leaders, based in Lusaka, are quite so scrupulous or so sophisticated in their dealings with representatives of capital or the regime remains to be seen. After such a lengthy period of exile and illegality the attractions of legitimacy must be many, but the ANC strategists have to weigh against that attraction the possibility of losing a section of their youthful supporters in the townships.

Black Majority Rule
The most likely scenario to emerge from the current powerful challenge to the regime and its increasing openness to political negotiation would be for a small opportunist element of the ANC to do a deal with the white minority government, on the basis of some power sharing arrangement in the urban areas, leaving the existing bantustans intact and the power base of the Inkatha Movement inviolate. However, such a partial solution is likely to be part of a continuing unstable equilibrium and in the long run it is likely that the centrist elements of the UDF and the mainstream of the ANC will link together once the ANC is legalised, or is sufficiently strong to operate in open defiance of the government. The next, perhaps optimistic, scenario amongst the many possible ones available is that such a coalition movement representing the generality of black and brown interests will inherit political power based on a non-racial franchise with a minimal degree of violence and electoral fraud. Assumption three, therefore, is that black majority rule will come to South Africa and that a broad base of black and brown South Africans will support a party comprising elements of the UDF and ANC. For the sake of argument, I shall call the party that might emerge from this alliance the United National African Party (UNAP).

Private Property and Collective Ownership
Because much popular commentary on South Africa depicts the black and brown population in an undifferentiated way, it is often assumed that all subordinated groups have a self-evident collective class interest which will be met by the destruction of apartheid. I have already indicated that black and brown South Africans have a variety of class interests to protect, maintain or defend. One line of fissure is between those with a rural landed base and the emergent professional and petit bourgeoisie in the towns. Another division of interest is between these strata and the broad mass of landless peasants, underpaid workers, migrants and the urban unemployed. These distinctions, which are concealed by the conventional racial form of political discourse, are reflected in the many and diverse organisations that are loosely held together in the UDF.

What should also be emphasised, however, is that the ANC is by no means as monolithic a body as government propaganda has, in the past, proclaimed. This can be observed even in the public documents of the Congress movement, including the key document of the movement, namely the Freedom Charter compiled at the 'Congress of Peoples' in a meeting in 1955 at Kliptown. Given the mythology that accompanies this document, it will almost certainly comprise an important part of the political programme of our fictitious party, the UNAP. Yet the document wavers uneasily between private property and collective ownership. This heritage of a respect for private property (reflecting the class interests of brown merchants and businessmen as well as the general respectable temperament of African nationalism at that time) and the contrary commitment to nationalisation (reflecting the influence of the Communist Party) will remain unresolved. UNAP, therefore, will come to power with promises like these, extracted from the 1955 Freedom Charter, more or less intact:

> The mineral wealth beneath the soil, the banks and monopoly industry shall be transferred to the ownership of the people as a whole.
> All people shall have equal rights to trade where they choose, to manufacture and to enter all trades, crafts and professions.
> Restrictions of land ownership on a racial basis shall be ended and all the land redivided amongst those who work it, to banish famine and land hunger.
> Freedom of movement shall be guaranteed to all who work on the land.

Neutralism Abroad
The fifth and final assumption is that the foreign policy profile and

90

general orientation of UNAP will be similar to that established by Mugabe in Zimbabwe. This implies a somewhat friendlier attitude towards the Soviet Union and other countries of the eastern bloc, an alliance with the non-aligned movement, but the re-entry of the country into the Commonwealth. These broad international realignments, however, will be more of a facade designed to demonstrate the radical credentials of some ex-ANC members previously allied to the communist movement. Behind that facade it will be business as usual. The giant multinationals like Anglo-American (which currently prospers in Zimbabwe, Botswana and Zambia, amongst other places) will continue to run the mining houses and the industrial combines. The bulk of foreign investment will continue to flow from Europe and North America, though there will be some readjustments of the shares coming from different countries (the proportion coming from Britain probably diminishing significantly). Trade, aid and investment links will continue to trap the UNAP leadership into old and familiar patterns. Gold and diamonds will be traded in London, Europe will take the bulk of exported fruit (provided agricultural wages can be kept low enough and agricultural production is not severely disrupted by land grabbing), while a similarly wide range of multinational companies will provide branch plant and subsidiary production. As the new black and brown bourgeoisie establishes itself through state patronage and privileged access to public goods, discretionary consumption of imported goods will be maintained at present levels or rise modestly. The need to secure foreign exchange to pay for these goods will, in turn, have conservative implications for domestic politics, as I further specify below.

THE FOUR PILLARS OF APARTHEID

In the first chapter of this book I argued that the structure supporting apartheid rested on four major pillars: (a) the exclusive right to centralised political power by white politicians elected by a white electorate; (b) the division of race relations along spatial lines; (c) the regulation and allocation of black and brown labourers to the factories, farms and mines of South Africa and (d) the continuance of social control in the urban townships surrounding the key loci of political and economic power. It is time now to assess to what extent the recent disturbances in South Africa have shaken these four pillars sufficiently hard to permit the structure to tumble to the ground.

White Political Power
In the case of the white monopolisation of political power there have been a number of constitutional changes establishing for brown South Africans institutions parallel to those of the white Parliament. In

addition, a number of 'independent' homelands have been granted at least the facade of political representation. Finally, Community Councils and other forms of black representation at an urban township level have been established. All these forms of representation, however, fall very far short of constituting effective representation for the majority of South Africa's population. Black views are still not heard effectively, the popular movements of the black and brown majority remain banned, and the key political institutions remain under the firm control of the Nationalist Party. Should my assumptions hold good, I would expect a national unicameral legislative assembly to emerge, perhaps with protected seats in the medium term for the brown and white ethnic minorities. Local government, particularly in the townships, will become more representative and more responsive to local needs. Despite white fears, I doubt that the level of black electoral participation will be very high, at least after the first election. (This seems to be confirmed by electoral counts in most African countries, which are often under 30 per cent.) The level of effective representation of whites in the central government is therefore likely to be higher than their proportion in the population would merit.

Spatial Relations
In respect of the territorial division of South Africa along racial lines, this was perhaps the most ambitious, and in the long run might prove the most intractable, of the legacies left by apartheid. Millions of people have been labelled and classified according to a sterile set of racial assumptions. They have been rehoused, removed, dumped and resettled in residentially exclusive zones. Rural blacks have acquired the label of ancient tribal and national entities and have been given small parcels of land on which to create experiments in limited power. Some of these have remained puppet entities totally conditioned by the whims of the white South African politicians. But even in such small entities, personal, familial, class, clan and organisational loyalties begin to develop around the new territorial space. It is difficult to imagine how a future black South African government can totally disassemble the bantustans and pretend that the Mantanzimas and Buthelezis do not exist. I doubt, therefore, whether it will prove possible to dismantle the more stabilised bantustans (KwaZulu, the Ciskei and perhaps the Transkei) and would anticipate that some territorial autonomy, with some loose federal link to the central government, will emerge. As to the white, brown and black spaces in urban areas, we would essentially see a shift from discrimination on the grounds of race to disadvantage on the grounds of class, income and wealth. As the fault lines of race are to a large degree coincident with the fault lines of class, the majority of blacks, for example in

Johannesburg, will continue to live in Soweto. There will of course be some changes too. Second-generation rich whites will have to make friends with their *nouveau riche* brown and black neighbours. Following existing changes, the amount of shared space will increase and will cover all shopping and recreational facilities, all public buildings, and, most importantly, schools, health centres and hospitals. Wealthy whites will nonetheless be able to create small new exclusive white spaces in country clubs and private societies where social snobbery and the level of subscriptions will keep out all but the most brash of the *hoi polloi*.

The Regulation of Labour

As to the regulation and control of the labour supply, if passes and influx control are not already phased out by the minority white government, they will be abolished by the incoming UNAP government. But, like the present government, the leaders of UNAP will face a certain inexorable logic that underpins the fundamentally exposed South African economy. If they want foreign exchange to undertake development programmes and service the consumer needs of the emergent black and brown bourgeoisie, the UNAP leadership will need to ensure the continuity of gold production, export farming and manufacturing. Whereas the labour market for manufacturing can be left to free competition (though massive programmes of skill acquisition will have to be initiated), few black workers will freely undertake agricultural labour or mining at the rate necessary to secure high and continuous foreign earnings. It is possible that a massive land reform programme will permit the development of an alternative set of food and export-crop farmers to emerge in the form of small black proprietors (a strategy promoted in Zimbabwe with some success) but, just as in Zimbabwe, in the short and medium term the UNAP government will have to rely on the white farmers. There is no escape, even in the long term, from the need for the mining capital and expertise provided by the existing companies. Given the need for foreign exchange and the dependence on gold, there will be no alternative but to rely on some compelling mechanism, such as that provided by the labour bureaux, to regulate and supply labour to the mines and farms. Of course, the system need not be administered with its present brutality, but that there has to be some regulatory apparatus is, on the surface of it, inevitable.

Social Control

Finally, a few comments on the question of social control. The disintegration of South Africa into a state of political chaos and lawlessness in the event of black rule is, of course, the nightmare feared by many white residents and the one frequently evoked by the

National Party to retain support. It would be unrealistic to imagine that a country born in violence after the Boer War, with a ruling class sustained partly by institutionalised violence, will suddenly find itself inhabited by serene angels bathing in the gentle light of majority rule. At the same time, the usual white assumption that a black government would signal a collapse into immediate disorder is predicated on some exaggerated African comparisons. The Congo and Uganda, which are normally identified, never had the level of skilled personnel, bureaucratic expertise, industrial familiarity, educational attainment and general attunement to the modern world already found amongst South Africa's black and brown population. It is doubtful indeed that the Afrikaners were any better equipped to take over the governance of a modern state in 1948. South Africa's strategic position and mineral wealth also mean that it will be inextricably linked as a peripheral capitalist power to the metropolitan and industrial world – unlike Uganda, where its few coffee beans can be purchased for the world markets from alternative sources.

The better comparison, therefore, is not a selected number of other African states, but the modern post-colonial states of South-East Asia, a number of which have successful modernised their state structures in order to find a more favourable position in the international division of labour. Reference to the South-East Asian pattern of development is also meant to suggest that, while I think the problem of law and order is exaggerated, I do not necessarily see the UNAP operating a particularly liberal democratic model of government. There will be serious threats to the new order from 'bitter-ender' whites, from black groupings loyal to conservative tribal entities, and from unemployed and underemployed black and brown youth frustrated when 'Freedom' brings them little. Above all, the UNAP government will have to face the problem of uncontrolled squatting. The apartheid state faced it by mass removals – a policy that will be difficult to sustain in view of the constellation of political forces behind the projected government. But it will certainly have to evolve an urban management strategy, perhaps combining elements of self-help with site and service schemes, to cope with the uncontrolled movements of people compelled by the existing impoverishment of agriculture to search for survival in the urban and industrial areas.

WILL APARTHEID LIE DOWN?

Unlike the conservative theories discussed above, I am convinced that legalised white minority rule in South Africa cannot survive. I have also made the admittedly optimistic, though I think not simple-minded, assumption that black majority rule can be formally instituted in South Africa, even though after a period of prolonged and continuing political unrest and instability.

But will such an achievement signify the end of apartheid? Those of us who watched the 'winds of change' blow through Africa in the 1950s and 1960s were perhaps inclined to go along with Nkrumah's quasi-biblical dictum, 'Seek ye first the political kingdom, and all else shall be added to it'. Nkrumah's overthrow and the collapse of his country, and other post-colonial states, into stagnation and continued crippling dependence on the metropolitian powers have now generated a more sceptical attitude to the achievement of state power alone. Of course, gaining hold of the instruments of state power is important and can be used as a means for social mobilisation and regeneration: no better example can be provided than the extraordinary rate of social mobility by Afrikaners suckled at the breast of the post-1948 state.

The achievement of state power does not, however, dislodge imbedded social structures, or alter the economic 'facts of life'. In tropical Africa, decolonisation signalled the formal end of empire; it did not prefigure substantive independence. Likewise, in South Africa, the achievement of black majority rule will not signify the end of apartheid, but its legal and formal abolition. The Freedom Charter boldly states 'All apartheid laws and practices shall be set aside' – the first is easy to achieve by proclamation, but the heritage of apartheid practices will not be so easy to root out and destroy.

A Reading Guide and Bibliography

The theory and practice of apartheid in South Africa have attracted a large volume of academic and political literature and any reading guide is bound to be highly selective. There are a number of instructive early accounts – some of which have attained the status of minor classics. Amongst these I would include Macmillan (1929), Marais's (1939) work on the 'Cape Coloureds', van der Horst's (reprinted 1971) account of labour conditions, De Kiewiet (1941), Patterson (1957), Carter (1958), Neame (1962), Roux's (reprinted 1964) pioneering attempt to write an account from the point of view of the subject population, Bunting (1964) and Simons and Simons (1969). Early accounts written by black people are infrequent, but notable exceptions are four books written by participants in black political and labour movements, the first three of which have been reissued – Kadalie (1970), Plaatje (1969), Nzula et al. (1979) and Luthuli (1962).

The accounts mentioned so far are nearly all historical and autobiographical. Beginning in the 1960s, accounts by anthropologists, sociologists and political scientists began to be more prominent. In particular, I would highlight the works of Wilson and Mafeje (1963), van den Berghe (1964; 1965), Kuper (1965), Rex (1971), Adam (1971; 1971a), Trapido (1971), Magubane (1979), Lacey (1981), Bundy (1979), Marks (1970), Wilson and Thompson eds (1969–71), Brandel-Syrier (1971), Johnstone (1976), Gerhart (1978) and Cock (1980). With the exception of the *Oxford History of South Africa* edited by Wilson and Thompson, which remains largely within the orthodox white liberal historiography, the remaining historical works mentioned are strongly influenced by contemporary social science currents. Again, however, we have to look largely to autobiographical accounts to directly establish the viewpoints of black people. Amongst the most powerful statements are those by Nkosi (1965), Mokgatle (1971), and Hermer ed (1980).

The vigour of race relations research in and on South Africa has depended greatly on the work of the Institute of Race Relations. The Annual Survey of the Institute, edited in recent years by Gordon (1978 et seq.) is an invaluable source. Other liberal and radical opinion has been kept alive by a dynamic journal, the *South African Labour Bulletin*, and somewhat more ephemeral student journals like *African Perspectives* (Witwatersrand), which, though somewhat unprofesssional in presentation, nonetheless attempt to come to grips with pressing political and social issues. A radical 'History Workshop' tradition has been promoted by the Centre of African Studies at the Univerity of the Witwatersrand. Representative works include Bozzoli (1979) and van Onselen (1982). Another important recent trend derives from the upsurge of interest in 'political economy'. A wide-ranging collection of such analyses can be found in Murray (1983), but see also ROAPE (1976) and Adam and Gilomee (1979). A scholar who has recently attempted to synthesise marxist and liberal analyses is Lipton (1985) whose lengthy chapter on 'The Changing Balance of Political Power' is thoughtful and balanced.

As to works more directly relevent to Chapter 1 of this book, a few theoretical accounts on the question of ideology can be strongly recommended, namely: Larrain (1979), Giddens (1979), Lukács (1971), Habermas (1971), Mannheim (1936) and Althusser (1969). Discussions of apartheid itself as an ideology can be found in Moodie (1975), Hepple (1967) and Pelzer (1966). Foreign policy implications of the ideology can be seen in Nolutshungu (1975), while an account 'from the Afrikaners' point of view' can be found in van Jaarsveld (1963).

When looking at apartheid as the ordering of spatial relations, we are dealing mainly with the work of social geographers, one or two of whom relate their work to contemporary theories of the international division of labour. A useful general reference containing arguments along these lines is Massey (1984). Despite its obvious relevance, South African geographers have not fully integrated this body of theory with their own analysis, though relevant material on spatial and racial relations can be found in Lemon (1976), Western (1981), Smith ed (1982), Board et al. (1970), Fair and Schmidt (1974) and Fair and Shaffer (1972). A notable attempt to show how space can be manipulated as a means of social control is found in Western (1984). A planner's account is provided by Bell (1973), while speculative spatial scenarios, usually accepting the apartheid framework, can be found in Botha (1978), Niddrie (1968), Africa Institute (1976) and Malherbe (1974).

Another major pillar of apartheid is the regulation and segmentation of the labour supply. Comparative studies of this question can be found in Cohen (1986), Cohen et al. (1979), and Portes and Walton (1981). On South Africa itself, a useful, though very detailed, account of the origins of the migrant labour system can be found in Levy (1982). Wilson (1972, 1972a) provides two solid books on the labour supply system to the mines. His neo-classical explanations can be usefully contrasted to Wolpe (1972). To these accounts we must now add Johnstone (1976), Burawoy (1976), Savage (1977), the Riekert (1978) report, Nattrass (1981), Murray (1981), SARS (1983) and Curtis (1984).

On the question of social control, see Cohen (1985). The increasing role of the military in internal security is described in Frankel (1984). Why urban areas in all countries frequently provide a site for political contestation is argued and debated in 'the new urban sociology'. Some important references to this debate are Castells (1975), Mingione (1981), Harloe and Lebas (1981) and Forrest et al. (1982). Again the influence of the new urban sociology within South Africa has been quite limited, despite the presence of the black townships as the major sites for encounter and resistance. There is, as a conseqence, no real engagement with this body of work though writings that pertain include Western (1981), Lange and van Wyk (1979), Dewar (1978), Hirson (1979), Proctor (1979), Cillie Report (1979) and Morris (1980).

The list of references that follows contains all the items bracketed in the main text of this book, together with those just referred to in my reading guide and a number of additional readings listed for their intrinsic merit or interest.

References

Adam, H. 1971, *Modernizing racial domination: South Africa's political dynamics*, Berkeley, University of California Press

—(ed) 1971a, *South Africa: sociological perspectives*, London, Oxford University Press

—(ed) 1983, *South Africa: the limits of reform politics*, Leiden, E.J. Brill

Adam, H. and H. Gilomee, 1979, *Ethnic power mobilised*, New Haven, Yale University Press

Africa Institute, 1976, *Black homelands in South Africa*, Pretoria, The Institute

African labour news, periodical published by the International Confederation of Free Trade Unions, Brussels

African perspectives, student journal, University of the Witwatersrand

Althusser, L. 1969, *For Marx*, London, Allen Lane

—1971, *Lenin and philosophy and other letters*, London, New Left Books

Bell, T. 1973, *Industrial decentralisation in South Africa*, Cape Town, Oxford University Press

Board, C. et al. 1970, 'The structure of the South African space economy,' *Regional studies*, vol. 4, no. 3

Botha, P. R. 1978, *South Africa: plan for the future*, Johannesburg, Perskor Publishers

Bozzoli, B. (ed) 1979, *Labour, townships and protest*, Johannesburg, Ravan

Brandel-Syrier, M. 1971, *Reeftown élite*, London, Routledge & Kegan Paul

Bundy, C. 1979, *The rise and fall of the South African peasantry*, London, Heinemann Educational Books

Bunting, B. 1964, *The rise of the South African reich*, Harmondsworth, Penguin Books

Burawoy, M. 1976, 'The function and reproduction of migrant labor: comparative material from southern Africa and the United States', *American journal of sociology*, vol. 85, no.5, pp. 1051–87

Callinocos, A. 1976, *Althusser's marxism*, London, Pluto Press

Carter, G.M. 1958, *The politics of inequality: South Africa since 1948*, New York, Praeger

Castells, M. 1975, *The urban question*, London, Edward Arnold

Cell, J.W. 1982, *The highest stage of white supremacy: the origins of segregation in South Africa and the American South*, Cambridge, Cambridge University Press

Chisholm, L. and P. Christie, 1983, 'Restructuring in education', in SARS, q.v.

Cillie Report 1979, *Report of the commission of inquiry into rioting in Soweto and elsewhere from 16 June 1976 to 28 February 1977*, vol.I, Pretoria, South African Government Printer

Claasens, A. et al. 1980, 'The reserve army, legislation and labour action in South Africa', *Africa perspective*, no. 14, summer

Cock, J. 1980, *Maids and madams: the politics of exploitation*, Johannesburg, Ravan

Cohen, R. 1986, *The new helots: migrants in the international division of labour*, Aldershot, Gower

Cohen, R. et al. 1979, *Peasants and proletarians: the struggles of third world workers*, New York, Monthly Review Press

Cohen, S. 1985, *Visions of social control: crime, punishment and classification*, Oxford, Polity Press

Cooper, C. 1981, 'Verdicts on South Africa's new labour act', *Africa Bureau*, document paper no. 27, London, African Publications Trust, November/December

Crapanzano, V. 1985, *Waiting: the whites of South Africa*, London, Granada

Curtis, F. 1984, 'Contradiction and uneven development in South Africa: the constrained allocation of African labour-power', *Journal of modern African studies*, vol.22, no.3, pp. 381–397

Davies, R. et al. 1984, *The struggle for South Africa*, vols. I & II, London, Zed Press

de Beer, C. et al. 1983, 'Health', in SARS, q.v.

De Kiewiet, C.W. 1941, *A history of South Africa, social and economic*, Oxford, Clarendon

Dekker, L.D. et al. 1975, 'Case studies in African labour action in South Africa, and Namibia (South West Africa)', in R. Sandbrook and R. Cohen (eds), *The development of an African working class*, London, Longman

Dewar, N. 1978, 'Spatial dimensions of political frustration and resentment in South African cities: the example of metropolitan Cape Town', Unpublished paper to a meeting of the *Association of American Geographers*, New Orleans

Du Preez, P. 1982, *Social psychology of politics: ideology and the human image*, Oxford, Basil Blackwell

Du Toit, D. 1981, *Capital and labour in South Africa: class struggles in the 1970s*, London, Kegan Paul International

Fair T.J.D. and C.F. Schmidt, 1974, 'Contained urbanisation, a case study', *South African geographical journal*, vol. 56, no.2, pp. 155–166

Fair, T.J.D. and N.M. Shaffer, 1972, 'Population Patterns and policies in South Africa, 1951–1960', in R.M. Prothero (ed), *People and land in Africa south of the Sahara*, London, Oxford University Press

Fanon, F. 1970, *Black skin, white masks*, London, Paladin

First, R. 1983, *Black gold: the Mozambican miner, proletarian and peasant*, Brighton, The Harvester Press Limited, and New York, St. Martin's Press

Forrest, R. et al. 1982, *Urban political economy and social theory*, Aldershot, Gower

Frankel, P. H. 1984, *Pretoria's praetorians: civil-military relations in South Africa*, Cambridge, Cambridge University Press

Furnivall, J.S. 1948, *Colonial policy and practice: a comparative study of Burma and Netherlands India*, Cambridge, Cambridge University Press

Gann, L.H. and P. Duignan, 1981, *Why South Africa will survive*, London, Croom Helm

Gerhart, G.M. 1978, *Black power in South Africa: the evolution of an ideology*, Berkeley, University of California Press

Giddens, A. 1979, *Central problems in social theory*, London, Macmillan

Golden City Press, weekly newspaper, Johannesburg

Gordon, L. 1978 et seq., *A survey of race relations in South Africa*, [Annual vol.], Johannesburg, South African Institute of Race Relations

Greenberg, B. and H. Giliomee, 1983, 'Labour bureaucracies', *South African labour bulletin*, vol.8, no.4, pp. 37–50

Guardian, The, daily newspaper, Manchester and London

Gurr, T.R. 1970, *Why men rebel*, Princeton, Princeton University Press

Habermas, J. 1971, *Towards a rational society*, London, Heinemann Educational Books

Harloe, M. and E. Lebas, 1981, *City, class and capital*, London, Edward Arnold

Hellman, E. and H. Lever, 1980, *Conflict and progress: race relations in South Africa 1929–1979*, London, Macmillan

Hepple, A. 1967, *Verwoerd*, Harmondsworth, Penguin Books

Hermer, C. (ed) 1980, *The diary of Maria Tholo*, Johannesburg, Ravan Press

Hill, C.R. 1964, *Bantustans: the fragmentation of South Africa*, London, Oxford University Press

—1983, *Change in South Africa: blind alleys or new directions?* London, Rex Collings

Hirson, B. 1979, *Year of fire, year of ash. The Soweto revolt: roots of a revolution*, London, Zed Press

Hughes, H. and J. Grest, 1983, 'The local state', in SARS q.v.

Hutmacher, B. 1980, *In black and white: voices of apartheid*, London, Junction Books

Innes, D. 1984, *Anglo-American and the rise of modern South Africa*, London, Heinemann Educational Books

IIE (Institute for Industrial Education), 1975 in R. Sandbrook and R. Cohen (eds), *The development of an African working class*, London, Longman

Isaacs, H. 1985, *Struggles within the struggle: an inside view of the PAC of South Africa*, London, Zed Press

Johnson, J. 1981, *Soweto speaks*, London, Wildwood House. Includes photographs by Peter Magubane

Johnson, R.W. 1977, *How long will South Africa survive?* London, Hutchinson

Johnstone, F. 1976, *Class, race and gold: a study of class relations and racial discrimination in South Africa*, London, Routledge & Kegan Paul

Kadalie, C. 1970, *My life and the ICU*, London, Frank Cass and Co., edited by S. Trapido

Koch, E. 1983, '"Without visible means of subsistence": slumyard culture in Johannesburg 1918–1940', in B. Bozzoli (ed), *Town and countryside in the Transvaal*, Johannesburg, Ravan Press

Kuper, L. 1965, *An African bourgeosie*, New Haven, Yale University Press

Lacey, M. 1981, *Working for Boroko: the origins of a coercive labour system in South Africa*, London, Ravan

Lambley, P. 1980, *The psychology of apartheid*, London, Secker & Warburg

Lange, J.H. and R. van Wyk, (eds) 1979, *Urban blacks in urban space*, Pretoria, School of Business Leadership, University of South Africa

Larrain, J. 1979, *The concept of ideology*, London, Hutchinson

Lea, J.P. 1982, 'Government dispensation, capitalist imperative or liberal philanthrophy? responses to the black housing crisis in South Africa' in D.M. Smith (ed) 1982, *Living under apartheid*, London, George Allen & Unwin

Legassick, M. and F. de Clerq, 1984, 'Capitalism and migrant labour in southern

Africa: the origins and nature of the system', in S. Marks and P. Richardson (eds), *International labour migration: historical perspectives*, Hounslow, Maurice Temple Smith

Lemon, A. 1976, *Apartheid: a geography of separation*, Farnborough, Saxon House

Levy, N. 1982, *The foundations of the South African cheap labour system*, London, Routledge & Kegan Paul

LL (*Lincoln Letter*), Newsletter published by the Lincoln Trust, London and Washington

Lipton, M. 1985, *Capitalism and apartheid: South Africa, 1910–1984*, Aldershot, Gower and Temple Smith

Lodge, T. 1983, *Black politics in South Africa since 1945*, London, Longman

Lukács, G. 1971, *History and class consciousness*, London, Merlin

Luthuli, A. 1962, *Let my people go: an autobiography*, New York, MacGraw Hill

Machiavelli, N. 1950, *The prince and the discourses*, New York, Random House

Macmillan, W.M. 1929, *Bantu, Boer and Briton: the making of the South African native problem*, London, Faber and Gwyer

MacShane, D. et al. 1984, *Power! black workers, their unions and the struggle for freedom in South Africa*, Nottingham, Spokesman

Magubane, B. 1979, *The political economy of race and class in South Africa*, New York, Monthly Review Press

Makgetla, N. and A. Seidman 1980, *Outposts of monopoly capitalism: southern Africa in the changing global economy*, London, Zed Press

Malherbe, P. N. 1974, *Multistan: a way out of the South African dilemma*, Cape Town, David Philip

Mannheim, K. 1936, *Ideology and utopia*, New York, Harcourt, Brace and World

Marais, J.S. 1939, *The Cape Coloured people: 1652–1937*, London, Longmans Green and Co.

Marks, S. 1970, *Reluctant rebellion: the 1906–1908 disturbances in Natal*, Oxford, Clarendon Press

Massey, D. 1984, *Spatial divisions of labour: social structures and the geography of production*, London, Macmillan

Mayer, P. (ed) 1980, *Black villagers in an industrial society: anthropological perspectives on labour migration in South Africa*, Cape Town, Oxford University Press

Mingione, E. 1981, *Social conflict and the city*, Oxford, Blackwell

Mokgatle, N. 1971, *The autobiography of an unknown South Africa*, London, C. Hurst

Montagu, A. 1972, *Statement on race*, London, Oxford University Press

Moodie T.D. 1975, *The rise of Afrikanerdom: power, apartheid and the Afrikaner civil religion*, Berkeley, University of California Press

Morris, P. 1980, *Soweto: a review of existing conditions and some guidelines for change*, Johannesburg, The Urban Foundation

Murray, C. 1981, *Families divided: the impact of migrant labour in Lesotho*, Cambridge, Cambridge University Press

Murray, M. (ed) 1983, *South African capitalism and black political opposition*, Cambridge, Mass., Shenkman

Nattrass, J. 1981, *The South African economy: its growth and change*, Cape Town, Oxford University Press

Neame, L.E. 1962, *The history of apartheid: the story of the colour war in South Africa*, London, Pall Mall Press

Niddrie, D.L. 1968, *South Africa: nation or nations?* Princeton, Van Nostrand

Nkosi, L. 1965, *Home and exile and other selections*, London, Longman
Nolutshungu, S.C. 1975, *South Africa in Africa: a study of ideology in foreign policy*, Manchester, Manchester University Press
—1982, *Changing South Africa: political considerations*, Manchester, Manchester University Press
Nzula, A. et al. 1979, *Forced labour in colonial Africa*, London, Zed Press, edited by R. Cohen
Omond, R. 1985, *The apartheid handbook: a guide to South Africa's everyday racial policies*, Harmondsworth, Penguin Books
Patterson, S. 1957, *The last trek*, London, Routledge & Kegan Paul
Pelzer, A.N. 1966, *Verwoerd Speaks*, Johannesburg, Afrikaanse Pers
Pheko, M. 1984, *Apartheid: the story of a dispossessed people*, London, Marram
Piven, F.F. and R.A. Cloward, 1971, *Regulating the poor: the functions of public welfare*, New York, Pantheon Books
—1972, *The politics of turmoil: essays on poverty, race and the urban crisis*, New York, Pantheon Books
Plaatje, S.T. 1969, *Native life in South Africa: before and since the European war and the Boer rebellion*, New York, Negro Universities Press
Popenoe, D. 1973, 'Urban residential differentiation: an overview of patterns, trends, and problems', *Social Enquiry*, vol. 43
Portes, A. and J. Walton, 1981, *Labor, class and the international system*, New York, Academic Press
Proctor, A. 1979, 'Class struggle, segregation and the city: a history of Sophiatown, 1905–1940', in B. Bozzoli (ed), *Labour, townships and protest: studies in the social history of the Witwatersrand*, Johannesburg, Ravan Press, pp. 49–89
Rex, J. 1971, 'The plural society: the South African case', *Race*, vol.12, no. 4
—(ed) 1981, *Apartheid and social research*, Paris, UNESCO Press
Rhoodie, N. (ed) 1978, *Intergroup accommodation in plural societies*, London, Macmillan
Richardson, P. 1984, 'Coolies, peasants, and proletarians: the origins of Chinese indentured labour in South Africa, 1904–1907', in S. Marks and P. Richardson (eds), *International labour migration: historical perspectives*, Hounslow, Maurice Temple Smith
Riekert 1978, *Report of the commission of inquiry into legislation affecting the utilisation of manpower*, (Chairman, P.J. Riekert), Pretoria, South African Government Printer
ROAPE 1976, 'Special issue on South Africa', *Review of African political economy*, no. 7
Roux, E. 1964. *Time longer than rope: a history of the black man's struggle for freedom in South Africa*, Madison, University of Wisconsin Press
SAG (South African Government) 1985, *South Africa: mainstay of southern Africa*, pamphlet issued by the Ministry of Foreign Affairs, Pretoria
SAN (*South African Newsletter*) 1985, periodic handouts from the South African Embassy, London
SARS (South Africa Research Service), *South African review I: same foundations, new facades?* Johannesburg, Ravan Press
Saul, J.S. and S. Gelb, 1981, *The crisis in South Africa: class defence, class revolution*, New York, Monthly Review Press
Savage, M. 1977, 'Costs of enforcing apartheid and problems of change', *African Affairs*, vol.76, no. 304, pp. 287–302
Schlemmer, L. 1983, 'Build-up to revolution or impasse?' in H. Adam (ed), *South Africa: the limits of reform politics*, Leiden, E.J. Brill
Sergeant, H. 1984, *Between the lines: conversations in South Africa*, London, Cape

Simons, H.J. and R.E. Simons, 1969, *Class and colour in South Africa: 1850–1950*, Harmondsworth, Penguin Books

Smith, D.M. (ed) 1982, *Living under apartheid*, London, Allen & Unwin

Sommer, R. 1969, *Personal space*, Englewood Cliffs, N.J., Prentice-Hall

South African Labour Bulletin, independent journal, Johannesburg

Southall, R. 1982, *South Africa's Transkei: the political economy of an 'independent' Bantustan*, London, Heinemann Educational Books

Stahl, C.W. 1981, 'Migrant labour supplies, past, present and future: with special reference to the gold mining industry', in W.R. Bohning (ed), *Black migration to South Africa: a selection of policy-oriented research*, Geneva, International Labour Organisation

Streek, B. and R. Wicksteed, 1981, *Render unto Kaiser: a Transkei dossier*, Johannesburg, Ravan Press

Sunday Times, The, weekly newspaper, London

Times, The, daily newspaper, London

Trapido, S. 1971, 'South Africa in a comparative study of industrialisation', *Journal of development studies*, vol. 7, no. 3, April

UNESCO 1952, *The race concept: results of an enquiry*, Paris, UNESCO Press

van den Berghe, P. L. 1964, *Caneville: the social structure of a South African town*, Middletown, Wesleyan University Press

—1965, *South Africa: a study in conflict*, Middletown, Wesleyan University Press

van der Horst, S. 1971, *Native labour in South Africa*, London, Frank Cass and Co.

van der Merwe, S. 1985, *And what about the black people?* Pretoria, Information Service of the National Party

van Jaarsveld, F.A. 1963, *The Afrikaners' interpretation of South African history*, Cape Town, Simondium

van Onselen, C. 1982, *Studies in the social and economic history of the Witwatersrand*, vol.1, *New Babylon*; vol.2, *New Nineveh*, London, Longman

Wages Commission, n.d., *Riekert: don't worry, everything's okay*, Mimeographed pamphlet, Students Representative Council, University of Cape Town

Weber, M. 1968, *Economy and society*, 2 vols., New York, Bedminster Press

Western, J. 1981, *Outcast Cape Town*, London, Allen & Unwin

—1984, 'Social engineering through spatial manipulation: apartheid in South African cities' in C. Clarke et al. *Geography and ethnic pluralism*, London, Allen & Unwin

Wilkinson, P. 1983, 'Housing', in SARS q.v.

Wilson, F. 1972, *Labour in the South African gold mines, 1911–1969*, Cambridge, Cambridge University Press

—1972a, *Migrant labour in South Africa*, Johannesburg, South African Council of Churches and SPRO-CAS

Wilson, M. and A. Mafeje, 1963, *Langa: the study of social groups in an African township*, Cape Town, Oxford University Press

Wilson, M. and L. Thompson, (eds) 1969–71, *The Oxford history of South Africa*, vol.I (1969), vol.II (1971), London, Oxford University Press

Wolpe, H. 1972, 'Capitalism and cheap labour-power in South Africa: from segregation to apartheid', *Economy and society*, vol.1, no.4, pp. 425–56

Index of Names